The WISDOM *of* JESUS

BIBLE WISDOM FOR TODAY

The WISDOM
of JESUS

REV. MARCUS BRAYBROOKE

Reader's
Digest

The Reader's Digest Association, Inc.
Pleasantville, New York • Montreal

A READER'S DIGEST BOOK
Conceived, edited, and designed by
MARSHALL EDITIONS
170 Piccadilly, London W1V 9DD

PROJECT EDITOR: JAMES BREMNER
ART EDITOR: HELEN SPENCER
PICTURE EDITOR: ELIZABETH LOVING
RESEARCH: MICHAELA MOHER
DTP EDITORS: MARY PICKLES, KATE WAGHORN
COPY EDITOR: JOLIKA FESZT
MANAGING EDITOR: LINDSAY MCTEAGUE
PRODUCTION EDITOR: EMMA DIXON
PRODUCTION: ROBERT K. CHRISTIE
ART DIRECTOR: SEAN KEOGH
EDITORIAL DIRECTOR: SOPHIE COLLINS

The acknowledgments that appear on page 96 are hereby made
a part of the copyright page.

First North American Edition

Library of Congress Cataloging in Publication Data

Braybrooke, Marcus.
    The wisdom of Jesus / Marcus Braybrooke.—1st North
American ed.
        p.   cm.—(Bible wisdom for today : v. 2)
    Includes bibliographical references and index.
    ISBN 0-89577-908-0
    1. Jesus Christ—Teachings. 2. Jesus Christ—Parables. 3.
Jesus Christ–Preaching. 4. Jesus Christ—Counseling methods.
I. Title. II. Series.
BS2415.B69   1997
232.9'54—dc20   96-30611
                                                            CIP

Origination by HBM Print, Singapore
Printed and bound in Italy by Chromolitho

*Pictures on the preliminary pages are: (page 1) the
Parable of the Dragnet, from a 19th-century British
stained-glass window; (page 2) shepherd's fields near
Bethlehem; (page 3) the Sea of Galilee; (page 5) the
procession of the wise wedding attendants, or "virgins,"
from a sixth-century Byzantine mosaic.*

CONTENTS

INTRODUCTION

During his ministry in Palestine about 2,000 years ago, Jesus traveled among the towns and villages, healing people and teaching them new spiritual truths. He taught in many different ways. Sometimes he put across his meaning with parables – stories or short illustrations in which concrete images drawn from everyday life conveyed his spiritual message. At other times he delivered sermons, or discourses, using a familiar form to convey often revolutionary ideas. Even in one-to-one encounters he taught, simultaneously proclaiming universal truths and touching individuals where they hurt most deeply. Sometimes he addressed only his closest followers, or disciples; sometimes he spoke to a crowd of people. He found his audiences from all walks of contemporary Palestinian society.

Jesus was put to death by the Roman authorities – abbetted by some Jewish religious leaders, who believed he was a blasphemer against God – probably some time in the early AD 30s. But his followers did not forget what he had done and said; in the second half of the first century, they wrote down what they considered to be the most significant moments in his life.

✝ The Gospel writers ✝

This story, told in separate accounts by four of Jesus' followers, became known as the Gospel ("Good News"). Because the versions written by Mark, Matthew, and Luke look at Jesus' ministry from a similar point of view, they are known as the Synoptic Gospels. The Gospel of John, thought by scholars to have been written later than the others, contains miracles and incidents that the other three Gospel writers omitted.

Each writer had his own structure and emphases, aiming his account at a particular readership. Mark's Gospel, for example, is thought to be the earliest and therefore to contain the closest record of what Jesus actually said. Some scholars believe that what he wrote was derived from the sermons of Peter, Jesus' foremost disciple. Matthew wrote for a mainly Jewish readership, drawing heavily on Old Testament references and prophecies, while Luke aimed his Gospel primarily at Gentiles. John's Gospel, which was also intended mainly for Gentiles, is more reflective than the other three.

To appreciate the teaching of Jesus, it is helpful to try to understand what Jesus intended it to mean to his contemporaries, as well as the interpretation put on it by the first Christians. Modern biblical

The symbols used in the panels on top of each page represent the four Gospel writers. The lion symbolizes Mark; the man, Matthew; the ox, Luke; and the eagle, John. The symbols show the Gospel sources for each story.

commentators think that the earliest believers sometimes adapted Jesus' sayings and stories to particular concerns relevant to their own current needs. In the parable about the Ten Wedding Attendants (pp. 58–59), for example, Jesus seems to have told his listeners that the kingdom of God – the reign of God on earth – was imminent. After Jesus' death and resurrection, however, the first Christian preachers seem to have adapted the story to warn the faithful to prepare themselves for the Second Coming of the Lord – the moment when Jesus would return again to inaugurate the end of the world.

✝ *Parables, sermons, and conversations* ✝

The teachings of Jesus that follow are divided into three sections. The first contains Jesus' parables, which he used to illustrate topics and themes, such as the nature of the kingdom of God, His compassionate mercy toward sinners, and the need to be prepared for the

Jesus is depicted as the Good Shepherd in this sixth-century Byzantine mosaic from Ravenna, northeastern Italy. Instead of being shown with a shepherd's crook, Jesus holds a cross, symbolizing his crucifixion.

Last Judgment. The second section consists of sermons and discourses that Jesus preached to his disciples and others in the district of Galilee and Jerusalem. Among these are the Sermon on the Mount, which contains the Beatitudes, the Lord's Prayer, and some of Jesus' best-known sayings. The third section consists of a selection of conversations Jesus had with various individuals. They include people from differing backgrounds and circumstances, such as Nicodemus, a learned Pharisee who came to talk to Jesus privately at night in Jerusalem, and a woman of Samaria, who met Jesus by a well.

Jesus' words provided inspiration to those who first heard them and are still relevant today. Christians of every generation have pondered their meaning and treasured their imagery and poetry, and they have inspired some of the finest Christian art, examples of which are shown in this book. Those who find the sayings and stories familiar may discover fresh insights. Those who read Jesus' words for the first time may find, like many before them, that his is the "message of eternal life [John 6:68]." ❖

The Church of the Beatitudes crowns a hill overlooking the Sea of Galilee. Its site marks the spot where, by tradition, Jesus gave his Sermon on the Mount (pp. 66–71), a discourse containing the core of his teaching.

THE PARABLES
OF JESUS

Although many Jewish teachers at the time of Jesus used stories to teach religious principles, Jesus' teaching stories stand above the rest for their originality and depth. About a third of Jesus' teaching, recorded by the four Gospel writers, takes the form of parables. The parable itself is a story that uses comparison to illuminate a spiritual truth, usually with images and examples taken from everyday life.

Some of Jesus' parables were illustrations that presented examples of model attitudes. The Good Samaritan (pp. 22–25), for example, who cared for a man who had been beaten and robbed, represents the paradigm of the loving neighbor. Jesus sometimes presented allegorical parables, in which the details of the story corresponded to specific people or situations. Thus, in the story of the Wicked Husbandmen (pp. 52–55), the servants represent the Jewish prophets, the tenants are the Jewish religious leaders, and the king stands for God. At other times, Jesus' parables were not really stories at all but rather similitudes – short comparisons between two objects or situations.

The parables recounted in this section embody Jesus' teaching on various subjects. They illuminate the nature of the kingdom of God or heaven (pp. 10–19); stress the need for persistence in prayer (pp. 20–21); demonstrate how to love a neighbor (pp. 22–25); and portray Jesus as the prime example of sacrificial love (pp. 26–27). They also describe God's never-failing love toward sinners (pp. 28–41) and the faithful's need to be ready for God's judgment. ❖

SEEDS *of* FAITH

The SOWER

MARK 4:1–20; MATTHEW 13:1–23;
LUKE 8:4–15

" Listen! Imagine a sower going out to sow.
Now it happened that, as he sowed,
some of the seed fell on the edge of the path, and the
birds came and ate it up. "

MARK 4:4

I N THE SYNOPTIC GOSPELS – those of Mark, Matthew, and Luke – Jesus told a number of parables about the coming of the kingdom of God. Because the word *kingdom* suggests a physical realm, it might better be translated as the "reign" or "rule" of God. Biblical scholars continue to debate when Jesus himself expected God's rule on Earth to come. Some of his followers evidently thought it would come soon after his death; some may even have expected it as the immediate climax of his ministry.

One of Jesus' best-known parables about God's kingdom is the story of the Sower, which, according to Mark and Matthew, Jesus told to a crowd assembled by the Sea of Galilee. A sower, he said, went out to sow seed. Some seed fell on the edge of a path, where birds ate it up. Some of it fell on rocky ground, where it sprang up, but because the soil was shallow, it withered beneath the scorching sun. Some fell into thorns, which grew up and choked it. But some fell into fertile soil and produced a good crop – "the yield was thirty, sixty, even a hundredfold."

When Jesus had finished telling the parable, his 12 disciples asked him what it meant. In reply, Jesus tried to explain to them why he taught in parables in the first place. He seemed to suggest

that by using the symbolic imagery of the parable, he wanted to challenge his hearers to make new spiritual discoveries. Perhaps he thought they might retain more effectively what they had to figure out for themselves than what they had been told explicitly.

† *The meaning of parables* †

The Gospel writers, or evangelists, also appear to suggest that because Jesus taught in parables, only some of his hearers responded to his message. Quoting the prophet Isaiah (6:9), the evangelists imply that only those who were willing to change their behavior as a result of hearing Jesus would understand the spiritual meaning of the parables.

Jesus went on to explain the meaning of the parable. The seed that was sown was the word of God. The places where it fell represented people's different responses to the Gospels. The hardened path, where the seed was eaten up by the birds, represented those who, as soon as they heard the word, had the message taken away by Satan. The rocky ground stood for those who at first welcomed the word, but gave up as soon as they were persecuted. The thorny ground stood for those in whom the word was choked by the worries of the

world. Finally, the good soil represented those who heard the word and yielded a harvest.

Jesus' explanation of the parable showed it to be an allegory – a story in which each individual detail stands for something specific. In fact, the majority of the parables of Jesus, like the parables of contemporary rabbis, are not allegorical. Instead, the whole story conveys a single point of comparison.

The parable of the Sower, like Jesus' other stories, uses imagery that would have been familiar to the people of ancient Palestine. At that

❖ *The Sower scatters seeds, in this painting by the 16th-century Dutch artist Pieter Brueghel. In Jesus' parable, the seed fell on various types of terrain, but only that which fell in fertile soil grew and flourished.*

time, most farmers sowed the seed by hand before lightly plowing it in. After the June harvest, a field was either plowed almost immediately and left until the time of sowing in November or December, or it was not plowed at all, but left so that animals could graze on the stubble. When the time for sowing came, the field was divided into strips. The sower scattered the seed – which he took from a sowing cloth hung about him, or from his outer garment, which was gathered up to form a pouch – with a wide swing of his arm over the width of a strip. A plowman then plowed it in, endeavoring to cover up the seed as quickly as possible. Even so, some of the seed was bound to be eaten by birds.

> **❝ *This, then, is what the parable means: the seed is the word of God*. ❞**
>
> LUKE 8:11

In parts of Palestine, especially in the hill country, the rocky substratum reaches up almost to the surface and is covered by only a thin crust of earth. In an unplowed field, it would be difficult to know exactly where these rocky areas were. Seeds that fell there, however, grew up especially quickly, because the soil with rock beneath it was particularly warm, and the thin top soil was quickly saturated when it rained. Because the sun in Galilee, even early in the morning, can be very hot, it would easily scorch such plants, which would not have roots because of the rocks.

✝ *A good crop* ✝

After the harvest, if the field's stubble had been left for cattle to graze on, there would have been thorns as well. When the time came for sowing, thorns would have dried up in the hot sun and become parched and tough. But their roots remained so that as soon as there was rain the thorns would quickly revive and choke the new grain. Despite all the hazards, some seeds did fall into good ground and produce a crop. The average ear of wheat was expected, it seems, to bear about 35 seeds, but sometimes 60 or even as many as 100 were counted.

The methods of farming used in the time of Jesus are still practiced in the Palestine region today. Using a traditional plow, a farmer prepares the land before sowing it.

Rocky terrain such as this is typical in Palestine. The seed that fell on the rocky ground grew, but because the soil was shallow, the plants withered in the fierce heat.

When Jesus first told the parable, he probably intended it as a way of encouraging his disciples, who may have been disheartened by the fact that some of those who heard his message responded to it with indifference or hostility. Although many of the seeds that the sower sowed were wasted, Jesus said, there would still be a good crop. In the same way, his words would often be ignored, but there would still be a rich spiritual harvest. He reinforced this idea with the parables of the Yeast and the Mustard Seed (pp.16–17).

This message of reassurance must also have been a comfort to the early church, which had to face widespread persecution. It has also cheered many Christians in subsequent generations: the faithful preacher of the Gospel cannot guarantee the results, but just as year by year God provides a harvest, so God's word will bear fruit. ❖

MESSAGE
—for—
TODAY

The parable of the Sower promises that the deeds of those who act in faithfulness will eventually grow and flourish whether or not the faithful see it happen.

Modern Western culture seems to cultivate the need for immediate gratification. By contrast, leaders of different religions have always urged people to be detached from whether or not their labors bear fruit: what is important is carrying out a task to the best of one's ability. The modern Indian spiritual teacher J. Krishnamurti, for example, likened his teaching to a perfumed flower. People might or might not smell it — but that was not the concern of the flower. Similarly, Pope John XXII used to say, "I do my best and leave the rest to God." If we act to the best of our ability, we should have patience to allow the results to flourish and equanimity if they do not.

A MIXED HARVEST

The WEEDS ❖ The DRAGNET

MATTHEW 13:24–30; 36–43; 47–50

❝ *Sir, was it not good seed that you sowed in your field?*
If so, where does the darnel come from? ❞

MATTHEW 13:27

T HE STORIES OF BOTH the Darnel (a type of weed) and the Dragnet concern the end of the world, according to Matthew's presentation. But Jesus may also have intended them to explain that although many seemed to reject his message without consequence, a reckoning would finally come.

† The Weeds †

Jesus recounted the parable of the Weeds immediately after the story of the Sower. He told his listeners that the kingdom of heaven could be compared to a man who sowed good seeds in a field. But at night, when everyone was asleep, the man's enemy came and sowed weeds among the wheat. When the new wheat sprouted, with the weeds among it, the man's laborers asked him where the weeds had come from. He told them that "some enemy" had planted them.

The laborers asked whether he wanted them to dig the weeds up, but the owner told them not to. Certain weeds resemble bearded wheat, and in the early stages of their growth are hard to distinguish from the crop. The owner was clearly afraid that because there were so many weeds, the wheat might be pulled up at the same time.

The owner of a field of wheat, at left, tells his laborers to remove and burn the weeds harmful to his crop, in this detail from a 19th-century British stained-glass window. ❖

Instead, he ordered that both wheat and weeds should be allowed to grow until the harvest. The reapers would then gather the weeds, bundle them up and burn them, and collect the wheat separately.

Although the parable of the Weeds is not found in the other Gospels, it is related in the apocryphal Gospel of Thomas, a second-century text that was not included in the official canon of the New Testament. Thomas's Gospel is valuable because it provides other versions of 11 of the parables that occur in the Synoptic Gospels – those of Matthew, Mark, and Luke. In this case, his version of the story of the Weeds is essentially the same as Matthew's, although it provides fewer details.

Unlike Thomas, Matthew attributes to Jesus an allegorical interpretation of the parable. According to this, it is the Son of man – a title often given to Jesus – who sows the good seeds, representing the subjects of God's kingdom. The weeds stand for those who are subject to the Evil One, the Devil, who sowed them. At the end of time, the Son of man will gather out of his kingdom all who have done evil and throw them into the furnace, while the upright will shine like the sun in the kingdom of their Father.

In fact, the story was probably an answer to the question – perhaps from some of Jesus' disciples – as to why God allowed the wicked to flourish. On another occasion (Luke 9:51–56), when two of Jesus' disciples met with rejection by the people of a particular village, they asked Jesus whether they should call down lightning to destroy them. But Jesus replied that judgment would happen in God's time.

✝ The Dragnet ✝

The short parable of the Dragnet makes the same point. The kingdom of heaven, Jesus said, is like a dragnet that is cast into the sea and catches all types of fish. Just as fishermen wait until they have brought their net to shore to sort out the edible from the inedible fish, so, when judgment comes at the end of time, God will sort the good from the evil: "The angels will appear and separate the wicked from the upright, to throw them into the blazing furnace, where there will be weeping and grinding of teeth." ❖

MESSAGE
—for—
TODAY

IN ALL WALKS and epochs of life, people exist who act primarily with integrity, and often from a foundation of faith, while others proceed from motives of greed, selfishness, and self-aggrandizement. Yet, like the farmer and the fishermen in the parables, who were content to let the good and the bad coexist for a time, it is often better to be patient with those who seem to be evil in their self-centeredness. Their apparent shortcomings may be due to immaturity or temporary personal circumstances. By giving them a chance, their virtues may develop or become apparent.

The pursuit of goodness can easily be sidetracked by the distraction of criticizing others. People can ultimately take responsibility only for themselves. Others are answerable to their consciences and to God.

The PRICELESS TREASURE

The MUSTARD SEED ❖ The YEAST
The TREASURE ❖ The PEARL

MARK 4:30–32; MATTHEW 13:31–33; 44–50;
LUKE 13:18–21

❝ *What is the kingdom of God like?…It is like a mustard seed which…grew and became a tree.* ❞

LUKE 13:18

I N THESE FOUR short but vivid parables, Jesus conveyed the mysterious but revolutionary way in which the kingdom of God operated and the immeasurable value it possessed for people who took part in it.

✝ The Mustard Seed and the Yeast ✝

Despite its small beginnings, Jesus declared, the kingdom was like a mustard seed that grows into a tree, or like yeast that leavens "three measures of flour." The mustard seed was proverbially regarded as the smallest of all seeds. Jesus' suggestion in the parable that it became the "biggest of shrubs" is an intentional exaggeration, but mustard bushes on the banks of the Sea of Galilee did sometimes grow to an impressive 8–10 feet (2.4–3 m).

Jesus' reference to birds coming to make their nests in the tree might have reminded his hearers of the tree in the book of Daniel (4:18), which stood for the kingdom of Nebuchadnezzar, with the birds representing the nations under his dominion. In the Gospels, however,

Jesus compared the kingdom of God to a mustard seed, which can grow into a sizable bush, such as this one growing near the Sea of Galilee.

the tree is the kingdom of God and the birds are the Gentiles. Some scholars have noted that in Matthew, after Jesus had told these parables, he no longer addressed the common people. He taught only his disciples from then on, and he may have been already looking toward Gentiles joining the church after his death and resurrection.

The parable of the yeast also exemplifies something small that expands to a considerable size – three measures of flour was enough to feed 160 people. Again, Jesus' intention was to convey the universal transformation that the kingdom would bring about.

✝ The Treasure and the Pearl ✝

Jesus also taught that the kingdom was worth any sacrifices it might ultimately demand. He illustrated this with two images – buried treasure and a pearl – that would have immediately suggested great material worth to his audience. In ancient times, before the days of banks, a common way of keeping money safe was to bury it, especially if the country was prone to periodic invasion by foreign troops. If the owner died before he could tell his

The beauty of pearls such as these, shown in their oyster shell, was as desirable to a merchant, Jesus said, as the kingdom of God should be to the faithful.

heirs where the treasure was buried, it might lie forgotten for years.

In his story about treasure, Jesus said that a man came across a treasure trove and buried it again to keep it safe until he was able to buy the field. Jesus did not raise the moral question of whether the treasure rightfully belonged to the owner of the field. His point was that the man who had found the treasure was happy to sell all his possessions to buy the field because he recognized the great worth of the treasure. If a person is prepared to go to such lengths to acquire material wealth, Jesus seems to say, how much more should the faithful be prepared to make sacrifices to obtain spiritual treasure.

Jesus illustrated the same point with the image of the pearl. Pearls were prized throughout the ancient world. The Egyptian queen Cleopatra is said to have possessed a pearl worth 6 million sesterces – about 2 million dollars in today's currency. Like the treasure finder, the pearl merchant in Jesus' example, symbolizing people of faith, was willing to sell everything he owned to possess a pearl of great value – that is, the kingdom of God, whose worth is inestimable. ❖

MESSAGE
—for—
TODAY

THIS GROUP OF parables refers specifically to living faithfully and, if necessary, sacrificially, to gain citizenship in the kingdom of God. But the day-to-day application of the principle is sometimes lost in the spiritual language.

Whatever the faithful do in life should be done as an act of faith. People who dedicate themselves to a worthy professional or private pursuit are often required to make a sacrifice of time, energy, money, or emotion.

Marriage and family life require enough time to nurture them. Those who seek out God or "the meaning of life" need time for quiet contemplation. To achieve anything worthwhile and enduring – not least a satisfactory relationship with God – it is necessary, as the pearl merchant did, to make large sacrifices for the pearl beyond price.

A FAIR WAGE

The LABORERS in the VINEYARD

MATTHEW 20:1–16

> ❝ *The men who came last have done only one hour, and you have treated them the same as us, though we have done a heavy day's work in all the heat.* ❞
>
> MATTHEW 20:12

THE STORY OF the Laborers in the Vineyard uses a specific situation to illuminate the idea that God's generosity is the same toward sinners who repent at the last hour as toward those who have served him faithfully for many years. A landowner, Jesus said, went out at dawn to hire laborers to work in his vineyard – a familiar occurrence in ancient Palestine, where day workers would gather in a town's marketplace, hoping that someone would come to offer them employment. A working day lasted from sunrise to sunset and was divided into 12 "hours," which were counted from sunrise onward.

In this case, at the third hour and again at the sixth, the landowner hired more workers. At the 11th hour, when he again went to the marketplace, he found men who were still waiting there, so he hired them, too.

In the evening, the master told his bailiff to pay the men. Whereas he had explicitly agreed to pay a denarius – a generous amount by the standards of the day – to those hired in the morning, he had promised a "fair wage" to the

Disgruntled laborers confront the landowner, in this detail from a 19th-century British stained-glass window. The love of God, Jesus said, extends to all who turn to him, at any stage of their lives.

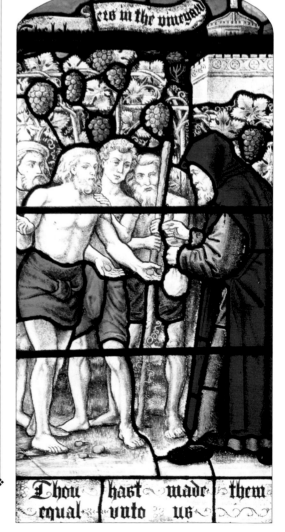

employees hired later. To those he had hired at the 11th hour, he had made no mention of pay – at least according to the more reliable biblical manuscripts. Presumably, all but the first hired expected a proportion of the day rate.

After everyone had been paid, those who had worked all day saw that the latecomers had each been given a denarius. Those hired early obviously hoped for extra. When they did not receive it, they complained to the landowner that they had worked longer and in worse conditions.

The landowner replied courteously, addressing the ringleader as "my friend," and explained that he had paid them what had been agreed at the outset. It was none of their business, he continued, what he did with his money and how much he paid the other workers: "Why should you be envious because I am generous?"

† *"The last will be first"* †

As with the story of the Prodigal Son (pp. 32–35), this parable was an answer to the criticism of some of the Jewish religious leaders, who questioned why Jesus welcomed sinners – the prostitutes, tax collectors, Samaritans, and other castoffs of society. Jesus replied that God showed the same generous mercy to all who turned to him, at any stage of their life. The story, however, made another point. It was a reminder to the self-righteous that everyone depends upon God's mercy. Those who have spent a lifetime in the service of the Master should have done so not in the hope of a greater reward than those converted late in their lives, but as a fitting response to God's goodness and mercy.

The parable ends with a more general conclusion, "Thus the last will be first and the first, last" – a saying that occurs in other contexts in the Gospels of Mark (10:31) and Luke (13:30). This suggests that the parable may have been retold among the first Christians as a warning to the disciples and leaders of the church not to allow their special position to be a cause of pride. ❖

MESSAGE
— for —
TODAY

IT IS NATURAL to feel a pang of annoyance when someone appears to be getting a better deal in life than we are. Likewise, it is easy to sympathize with the workers who had spent all day toiling in the heat and who received the same payment as those who had been hired in the evening. But there will always be people who are better paid, who have better health, more talent, or happier circumstances than ourselves.

Jesus taught that it is fruitless to compare oneself with others. God is generous to all His children, although in human, temporary terms, we may not see the nature of God's gifts. People will find the deepest joy when they concentrate on appreciating their own gifts with gratitude, instead of brooding on whether someone is more successful than they are – an attitude that will finally breed only discontentment.

The NEED for PERSISTENCE

The UNSCRUPULOUS JUDGE ❖
The IMPORTUNATE FRIEND

LUKE 18:1–8; 11:5–8

❝ *Pray continually and never lose heart.* ❞

LUKE 18:1

R ELATED ONLY IN Luke's Gospel, these two parables teach the value of sustained prayer and trust in God's loving care. They also illustrate one of Jesus' classic sayings: "Ask, and it will be given to you; search, and you will find [Luke 11:9]."

✝ The Unscrupulous Judge ✝

In the story of the Unscrupulous Judge, Jesus described how a widow came to a judge for justice against her enemy. For a long time he refused to grant her request, but eventually, worn down by her pestering, he gave in to her demands. Jesus ended the story by saying, "Now, will not God see justice done to his elect if they keep calling to him day and night."

In ancient Israel, the duty of a judge was to pronounce justice in the name of God (2 Chronicles 19:6). But the judge in the story is said to have had no fear of God nor respect for other people. One of the chief responsibilities of judges was to guarantee justice for orphans and widows, who, without husbands to protect them,

The neighbor who was awoken by the importunate friend would have lived in a house similar to this reconstruction of an ancient Palestinian dwelling.

were easy prey to exploitation. The justice of this woman's complaint was not in dispute. All she needed was a hearing. It was up to the judge to set the date for it. But only by her perseverance could the widow force him to give her justice.

The parable states plainly that if even an unjust judge will act when persistently asked, surely a loving God will take notice of the cries of His children. The logical extension of this, that God will act when human judges may not, must have comforted Christians in times of persecution.

✝ The Importunate Friend ✝

Jesus made the same point in the parable of the Importunate Friend, also known as the Friend at Midnight. He told of a man who, on receiving an unexpected, late visitor, went to a nearby friend in the middle of the night to ask for bread to feed his guest. Although the neighbor at first refused his request, Jesus said that the man's persistence would eventually prevail.

The story gives small insights into village life in Jesus' time. There were no stores, and in every home the woman of the house would rise early to bake the day's supply of bread for her family. It was probably generally known which families typically had some bread left over in the evening. The neighbor was annoyed at being disturbed and showed his irritation by omitting the customary greeting, "friend," from his reply. He explained why he could not help: he had already bolted the door, and it would have been tiresome to open it.

In a one-room peasant's house, the whole family slept together. Everyone would have been disturbed if the man had gotten up and started searching for bread in the semidarkness. Yet even if the neighbor would not respond to the request for friendship's sake, Jesus said, he would be forced out of bed by his friend's persistent calling. So if even a reluctant neighbor gave in to the relentless demands made upon him, how much more readily would a loving heavenly Father answer the prayers of the faithful? ❖

MESSAGE
—for—
TODAY

PEOPLE WHO PRAY to God with a shopping list of requests they want Him to supply often give up their practice of prayer if they feel God is not addressing their concerns soon enough. Both these parables, however, teach the importance of persistence and faith in prayer. The widow and the friend who needed bread kept asking because they had confidence in the outcome. People must not be deterred by an apparent lack of response.

Jesus stated that God will certainly answer our prayers. If an answer is not evident, it may be that God has heard the prayer, but we have not listened to His answer. If we accept that God knows our needs better than we do, we must allow Him to respond to our prayers as He sees fit. Sometimes it is only years after we have prayed for something that we realize that God did indeed hear or listen to our petitions.

A COMPASSIONATE TRAVELER

The GOOD SAMARITAN

LUKE 10:24–37

*" A man was once on his way down from Jerusalem
to Jericho and fell into the hands
of bandits; they stripped him, beat him, and then
made off, leaving him half dead. "*

LUKE 10:30

JESUS TOLD THE story of the Good Samaritan, one of the best known of his parables, during a conversation with a lawyer. Luke says the lawyer had asked Jesus what he should do to inherit eternal life. Jesus replied by asking him what was said in the Torah, which, although often translated as the Law, really means the whole teaching of God. The lawyer said that it called for wholehearted love of God and of one's neighbor. He then asked Jesus, "And who is my neighbor?" Instead of giving a strict definition, Jesus chose to tell him this story.

A man was traveling on the road from Jerusalem to Jericho when he was attacked by bandits, who robbed him and left him half dead. A priest and a Levite, or temple official, saw him lying there but passed by on the other side of the road. In contrast, a Samaritan – a man from Samaria in northern Palestine – stopped, looked after him, and took him to an inn. It was this Samaritan, Jesus suggested, who acted in the way a neighbor should.

In the ancient world, a line was often drawn between those who were considered "insiders" and those who were "outsiders." In Israel, for example, it was permissible to charge a "foreigner" interest, but not your "brother." Who was – or was not – a brother or neighbor or foreigner was therefore of some financial importance. Also, at the time of Jesus, Romans, Greeks, Syrians, and Samaritans together shared the land of Israel with the Jews. So the lawyer was probably genuinely curious as to whom Jesus would classify as a neighbor.

† The priest and the Levite †

Those who heard Jesus' story would have recognized the situation described. The road from Jerusalem to Jericho was notoriously dangerous. Jerusalem lies more than 650 feet (200 m) above sea level, and the road drops steeply in its 35-mile (55-km) descent to Jericho, which is situated 820 feet (250 m) below sea level. The road passes through wild, rocky, unpopulated country. Anyone left badly injured along the way would have had little hope of survival unless help happened to come quickly.

The parable gives no explanation of the priest's and Levite's behavior. They may have feared that contact with a dead body would have made them

ritually impure, as the Jewish Law stated. But since they were coming down from Jerusalem, this would not have interfered with their religious duties at the Temple. Luke implies that they deliberately crossed to the other side of the road to avoid the stricken victim. By contrasting this action with the Samaritan's compassion, Luke makes it clear that it is this quality that the priest and the Levite were lacking.

Jesus' listeners might have expected the story to contrast the kindness of a Jewish lay person

❖ *The Samaritan tends to the wounds of an injured man, in this painting by the Victorian English artist William James Muller. In the story, Jesus contrasted the compassionate nature of the Samaritan with the behavior of the priest and Levite who avoided the suffering man.*

with the two religious figures. Certainly, the mention of a Samaritan would have been a shock to them. Jews avoided the Samaritans and did not regard them as belonging to the chosen people. They were not "neighbors." This distinction had its root in the time when the Assyrians destroyed the northern kingdom of Israel and its capital, Samaria, in about 722 BC and deported many Israelites. Those who were left eventually mingled and intermarried with the pagan people who were settled in the land and adopted their religious practices (2 Kings 17). It was these people who in Jesus' time were known as Samaritans.

✝ The priest and the Levite ✝

In 593 BC the Babylonians conquered Jerusalem, capital of the southern kingdom of Judea, and deported the Jews to Babylon. From 538 BC, when the Jews began to return to Jerusalem from

The road from Jerusalem to Jericho winds through rugged terrain. In Jesus' time, people making the journey between the two cities ran the risk of being robbed. Even today the road can be a daunting prospect for travelers.

exile, they refused to recognize the Samaritans and rejected those who wanted to help with the rebuilding of the Temple. The Samaritans then built their own temple on Mount Gerizim in the north of Palestine.

> **❝ *A Samaritan traveler who came on him was moved with compassion when he saw him. He went up to him and bandaged his wounds...* ❞**
>
> LUKE 10:33–34

Jews avoided any contact with the Samaritans. Yet in the parable it was a despised Samaritan who helped the victim, who could be inferred to be a Jew. The Samaritan cleaned the man's injuries with oil and wine – the customary treatment for

A modern-day Samaritan farmer tends his field in Samaria, northern Palestine. In Jesus' time, Samaritans were considered schismatic outsiders by the Jews.

wounds. He bandaged the man up, put him on his own mount, and took him to an inn, where he looked after him.

The next day, when the Samaritan had to resume his journey, he gave the innkeeper the equivalent of two days' pay to look after the injured man. Clearly the innkeeper felt he could trust the Samaritan, since he took his word that he would be recompensed for any extra expense.

At the end of the story, Jesus asked the lawyer who he thought had been a neighbor to the man who had been attacked. The lawyer said it was the man who had shown pity. "Go, and do the same yourself," Jesus said. By challenging the divisions between the Jews and Samaritans, Jesus made it clear that anyone who responds to someone in need of help is a neighbor. ❖

MESSAGE
—for—
TODAY

MANY PEOPLE *put a limit on their compassion. They may believe that acts of charity begin — and end — at home. They may be satisfied with giving set amounts of money or time to select causes. But this parable teaches that compassion is not something that can be switched on or off. The Samaritan could have felt justified in continuing his journey once he had dressed the victim's wounds. Instead, he took him to an inn and paid for his stay.*

Compassion, which literally means "suffering with," is a state of being that gives people the capacity to respond to anyone in need, irrespective of their nationality, creed, race, or color. Jesus consistently tried to put across this message during his ministry. Beggars, prostitutes, Gentiles, Samaritans — no one was excluded from God's loving concern.

CARING *for the* FLOCK

The GOOD SHEPHERD

JOHN 10:1–18

> ❝ *I am the good shepherd; I know my*
> *own and my own know me, just as the Father*
> *knows me and I know the Father;*
> *and I lay down my life for my sheep.* ❞
>
> JOHN 10:14–15

ACCORDING TO JOHN'S Gospel, some time when Jesus was visiting Jerusalem, he cured a man who had been born blind. He performed this healing on the Sabbath – the day of rest. Afterward, in answer to some of the Pharisees who criticized him for working on the Sabbath, Jesus told a parable in which he used imagery drawn from contemporary sheep farming to illustrate his devotion to his followers and his readiness to sacrifice himself on their behalf.

The first image Jesus evoked was that of a thief trying to climb into a sheepfold – a scenario he contrasted with that of a shepherd who entered through the gate. The shepherd's voice, Jesus said, would be recognized by his sheep, and they would follow only him.

Jesus' audience would have been familiar with this scene. In Palestine at that time, sheep were usually brought into a courtyard in front of a house in the evening. Several flocks belonging to different people were sometimes kept in the same fold, and a gatekeeper was employed to watch over them at night. Whereas shepherds were let in at the gate by the gatekeeper, anyone trying to climb into the fold was certain to be a robber. Inside the fold, the shepherd would call to his sheep, who would respond to his voice – they would never follow other shepherds or strangers.

Jesus is depicted as the Good Shepherd carrying his beloved sheep in this painting by the 16th-century German artist Abel Grimmer. Jesus used the images of the shepherd and sheep to illustrate his loving care and commitment toward his followers.

The Pharisees did not grasp the story, so Jesus explained by telling them that he himself was "the gate of the sheepfold." He was referring to a situation when, if it was too far to bring a flock of sheep back home, a shepherd would drive the sheep into a nearby cave or temporary sheepfold. He would then lie down for the night across the entrance, acting as a sort of gate. A person could gain access to the sheep only by climbing over the shepherd and waking him up.

Jesus made another contrast between a thief, who came only to kill and destroy the sheep, and his own loving care for them. Anyone, he said, who entered the fold through him would be safe and live life to the full. He then contrasted the "good shepherd" with hired men who had no love for their sheep and readily abandoned them when they saw a wolf coming. He, however, was willing to lay down his life for his sheep – in other words, his people.

That he would surrender his life, he said, was the reason why his Father loved him. And his sacrifice, he emphasized, was his free choice in obedience to his Father's will.

✝ The Father, Jesus, and the faithful ✝

Jesus' parable echoes the images of sheep farming that are found in the Old Testament in both a positive and a negative sense. On one hand, in Ezekiel 34, the Jewish rulers are compared to shepherds who have neglected and exploited their flocks. On the other, in Psalm 23, the Lord is spoken of as a shepherd whose sheep lack nothing: "In grassy meadows he lets me lie. By tranquil streams he leads me…"

By using these familiar images, Jesus sought to explain the close relationship between himself and God the Father, as well as his care of, and sacrificial commitment to, the faithful. Jesus also referred to other sheep "that are not of this fold," who would also hear his voice. Presumably, this was an allusion to the fact that Gentiles would also become believers. ❖

MESSAGE
— for —
TODAY

THROUGH HIS IMAGERY of the good shepherd and his flock, Jesus illustrated the relationship that existed between himself and the faithful. He presented an ideal model of any relationship that involves a leader and followers.

Parents, managers of sports teams, senior executives, teachers — all need to establish a bond of trust between themselves and their charges, based on selfless concern for those charges. If leaders are in their position simply because of money, status, or power, they may well, like the hired men in the parable, abrogate their responsibility when the going gets tough. A true leader will be prepared to make sacrifices, just as Jesus was ready to give up his life for humankind. Jesus did it perfectly and was perfectly trustworthy. He suggested that those who follow him can trust him to help them live up to this ideal.

The PLACE of HUMILITY

The PHARISEE and the TAX COLLECTOR ❖
The LOWEST SEAT at the FEAST

LUKE 18:9–14; 14:7–14

" The tax collector stood some distance away, not daring
even to raise his eyes to heaven; but he beat his
breast and said, 'God, be merciful to me, a sinner.' This man,
I tell you, went home again justified... "

LUKE 18:13–14

THROUGHOUT HIS MINISTRY, Jesus emphasized to his listeners that God's mercy was available to everyone who genuinely turned to Him, whether they were priests or beggars. What was important was a person's humble attitude toward God, – not his or her societal status or outward piety. The parables of the Pharisee and the Tax Collector and the Lowest Seat at the Feast both teach the virtue of humility. But they also present a thinly veiled criticism of the behavior of some of the Pharisees.

✝ The Pharisee and the Tax Collector ✝

This story tells of an upright Pharisee and a tax collector who both went to pray at the Temple. The Pharisee's prayer expressed gratitude to God for allowing him to live a righteous life; for not being "grasping, unjust, adulterous;" and for fasting and paying his tithes. The tax collector, by contrast, simply cried out, "God, be merciful to me a sinner." It was the tax collector, Jesus said, who went home "justified."

To appreciate the full impact of both parables, and the nature of Jesus' disputes with some of the Pharisees, it is helpful to look behind the

traditional image of the Pharisees as being proud and hypocritical religious men. The origins of the Pharisaic movement are uncertain, but by the first century BC its adherents were instrumental in bringing about a number of far-reaching changes in the Jewish religion.

Among other precepts, the Pharisees taught that religion was not simply a matter for the priests at the Temple in Jerusalem: each Jew had to enter into a personal relationship with God, who watched over and cared for each individual. They also stressed that people should try to follow a pure and disciplined way of life; but, some of them, in their strict observance of the Torah (Law), seem to have become an exclusive, overly critical group.

Jesus, by contrast, mixed freely with ordinary people and made a point of seeking out the disreputable members of society – adulterers, prostitutes, and those in the pay of the occupying Roman Empire. In doing this, Jesus bypassed the normal Jewish requirement for repentance and pardon provided by the Temple rituals. Instead, he proclaimed that God took the initiative in seeking those who were lost; he justified his own ministry to society's castoffs by an appeal to the character of God.

Jesus' contemporaries would probably have regarded the Pharisees with respect, although glad enough to poke fun at them. The Pharisee in the parable seems to have been genuinely devout. Every Jew was expected to fast once a year on the

The Pharisee, at left, thanks God for his virtues, while the tax collector asks to be forgiven for his sins, in a detail from a 19th-century stained-glass window at Lincoln Cathedral, England. The tax collector's humility pleased God, Jesus said, more than the Pharisee's piety.

Roman aristocrats enjoy a banquet, in this AD first-century Roman relief from Trier, Germany. Banquets similar to this one would have been held in ancient Palestine at wedding celebrations and on other festive occasions.

Day of Atonement, but this man apparently fasted twice a week. Jews were also expected to give a tithe – one-tenth of their produce – to the service of God. Any wine or corn that a person purchased was usually assumed to have been already tithed by its producer, but this Pharisee had taken no chances and had even given tithes of everything he had bought.

✝ Collaborators with Rome ✝

The story contrasts the Pharisee with a tax collector. In Roman-occupied Palestine, tax collectors were particularly unpopular. They had to raise a set amount of taxes from a specified area, and they took a large commission. Their work also meant they had to collaborate with the hated Roman authorities.

When Jesus described the tax collector as "standing some distance away" and "not daring even to raise his eyes to heaven," his listeners probably thought that Jesus had put him in the place where he belonged. Yet the man's prayer in the temple, "God, be merciful to me, a sinner," was simple and humble and meant that he went home "justified" – a word that here seems to mean "at peace with God" – with the assurance of forgiveness.

Jesus' generalized conclusion to the story – "everyone who raises himself up will be humbled, but anyone who humbles himself will be raised up" – is also found at the end of the parable he told about avoiding the place of honor at a celebratory banquet. This parable also focuses on the necessity for humility.

✝ The lowest seat at the feast ✝

Jesus told this story at a dinner to which he had been invited by one of the leading Pharisees. Although it was the Sabbath, the day of rest, Jesus had just healed a man suffering from dropsy – a condition of excessive bodily fluid.

Noticing how the guests had picked the places of honor at the table, Jesus warned them that when people were invited to a marriage feast they should avoid these seats; otherwise, to their embarrassment, they might be asked by the host to move to a lower place to make room for a more important guest. If a person chose the lowest place, however, the host might invite him to move his place to a higher position, and everyone would see how honored he was.

> ❝ No; when you are a guest, make your way to the lowest place and sit there, so that, when your host comes, he may say, 'My friend, move up higher.' ❞
>
> LUKE 14:10

Similar illustrations about humility can also be found in various Jewish writings. In the Book of Proverbs, for example, it says: "In the presence of the king do not give yourself airs, do not take a place among the great; better to be invited, 'Come up here,' than be humiliated…[25:6–7]."

Here, Jesus used a social occasion and the fear of embarrassment to illustrate the need for humility. By implication, he criticized those who expected the best seats in heaven. At the same time, his criticism vindicated his own ministry, which led him to mix with all types of people because his message of God's mercy was for everyone. ✦

MESSAGE
—for—
TODAY

PEOPLE OFTEN BOOST their own egos by focusing on the presumed faults of others. But as the parable suggests, even the most wretched or despised people can experience a change of heart, recognize the error of their ways, or regain a sense of purpose in life. The path of righteousness often leads to arrogance; recognition of one's shortcomings can lead to humility and repentance.

Jesus made it clear that humility is an indispensable attitude for anyone who wants to follow him. He showed this graphically when, according to John 13, he insisted on washing his disciples' feet, shortly before his arrest, trial, and execution. He also made it plain that, contrary to the values of the world, where kings and rulers are most honored and the poor and destitute least recognized, the kingdom of God operated on the opposite principle.

RETURNING to the FATHER

The PRODIGAL SON
LUKE 15:11–32

> *" I will go to my father and say: Father, I have sinned against heaven and against you; I no longer deserve to be called your son. "*
> LUKE 15:18–19

ALTHOUGH KNOWN as the Prodigal Son, this parable might be called the Prodigal Father, who was prodigal, or extravagant, in his love toward his repentant son. Jesus intended the story to emphasize the outgoing love of God, who, like the father in the parable, does not wait until a sinner has made a formal act of penitence but goes out to greet him while he is still far off.

The story concerns two sons, the younger of whom asked his father for his share of the inheritance. When he had received his money, he went off to a distant country, where he frittered all his money away on a life of debauchery. Eventually, his money ran out and he was so destitute that he was forced by necessity to take a job feeding pigs.

The son realized that he would be better off as a servant working for his father. So he made his way back home. When he was still some distance from the house, he was spotted by his father, who ran out to greet him and ordered that he be given a robe, a ring, and sandals. To celebrate his son's return, the father then arranged a grand feast, for which a fattened calf was slaughtered.

The elder brother, however, resented all the attention lavished on his sibling. He complained to his father that he had dutifully worked for him for years, but had never been given the chance to celebrate with his friends. His father explained to him that it was only right to rejoice in the fact that his brother who was "dead" had come to life.

The parable not only bears a powerful message about the nature of love and compassion, but also sheds light on life in Jesus' time. It would not have been unusual, for example, for a younger son to ask for his share of the inheritance. By law, a farm was a family possession and passed from father to eldest son, but any younger sons had a right to a share of the disposable property.

The younger son's decision to go and live in a "distant country" was not necessarily a sign of rebellion against his father. By the time of Jesus, Jews had settled in many parts of the Mediterranean world. This diaspora, or "dispersion," has been estimated at about 4 million – whereas only about half a million Jews lived in Palestine itself. The son could easily have sought out one of these Jewish settlements.

+ A life of debauchery +

When the son reached his destination, he lived an immoral life and wasted all his money. Instead of seeking help from the nearest Jewish community, he accepted work from a Gentile looking after pigs – animals that Jews regarded as unclean. Presumably he must have

The prodigal son returns to the embrace of his father, in this detail from a 16th-century German altarpiece. God, Jesus said, will welcome the repentant sinner in the same way. Other scenes from the story are also shown: the son feeding the pigs, at left, and the celebratory banquet.

Jhefus fagt difze gleychnus Em mesch
hat zwe sun/ vnd d'jüngst begert sein teyl erb/ vnd als ers hatt/ vertheit ers
mit praßen/ fieng an armūt leydē/ müst d'schwei hüttē vn begert sei bauch
zefullē mit trestern die die schwei assen/ rc. Da schlüg er in sich selbs/ vn spich
wie vil taglöner habē brots gnüg in meins vatters hauß/ vnd ich verdirb im
hunger/ Ich will hingee/ zu meine vatter sag/ Vatter ich hab gesundiget in
dem himel vnd vor dir/ vnd bin fürre nit werdt das ich dein san heyß
mach mich als ein taglöner/ Vnd macht sich vff/ vnd kam zu seine vatter
vnd der vatter empfieng m mit fröude/ bekleydt in
macht im wurtschafft/ mit seinē freu
den/ Aber der elter bru
der murret darwider/
der vatter stillet in
rc.   rc.

Luce.
15.

earned something for looking after the pigs, but not enough to stop him from feeling hungry. It is not clear why he did not eat the "husks" – which would have been carob beans – that were fed to the pigs. Perhaps his employers forbade him to eat them, or possibly the association of the husks with swine repulsed him.

† *The son's return* †

According to an ancient Jewish proverb, "When the Israelites stand in need of carob beans, then they return to [God]." Certainly, it was the son's hunger that prompted him to return home and regret his wayward life. In his new determination to return, he prepared himself to confess to his father, "Father, I have sinned against heaven and against you."

The son was still a long way off when his father first saw him. Had his son been closer, the father would have seen that the boy was in a wretched state. The details of the story emphasize how delighted the father was at his son's return. It would have been considered undignified for such a man in that time to be seen running, yet the father ran to meet his son.

By clasping him in his arms, he prevented his son from going down on his knees and humbling himself. Kissing him on the cheek showed that the son was still part of the family and also of equal standing. No master kissed his servants and slaves, and they would kiss only the master's feet.

The giving of the ring bestowed authority; shoes, which were a luxury, distinguished the free man from the slave; and the killing of a fattened calf showed that the feast would be lavish. If a human father behaved toward his erring son in this manner, how much more, Jesus suggested, would the heavenly Father, in His infinite love, show pity on a sinner?

The husks that the destitute son fed to the pigs are believed by scholars to be pods (below) from the carob tree (right). The tree grows in Palestine and other parts of the Mediterranean region.

It is the second half of the parable that particularly challenged Jesus' Jewish opponents. In criticizing his message of forgiveness to sinners, they were behaving, in effect, like the elder son.

† *"You are with me always"* †

By the time the elder son came back from the fields, he could hear the music and dancing that customarily followed the end of a feast. When the elder son found out the reason for the celebrations, he was angry and refused to go inside the house. His father came out to persuade him, but the son angrily replied that he had slaved away for many years, and never once had he been offered so much as a baby goat for a feast with his friends.

To this rebuke the father gently replied, "My son, you are with me always, and all I have is yours." Like the vineyard owner in the parable of the Laborers (pp.18–19), who paid the same amount to workers he hired at different hours of the day, the father was not being unfair or unjust.

> **" But it was only right we should celebrate and rejoice, because your brother here was dead and has come to life; he was lost and is found. "**
> LUKE 15:32

Jesus told this parable to illustrate the abundant love of God for sinners who turn to him. In so doing, he also intended to answer the Pharisees' criticism that he never turned away the destitute and dissolute who came to hear or see him. Jesus did not deny God's care for the Pharisees, but, at the same time, he insisted that God has the same concern for those who have turned their back on him. When, in their own time, they return, it should naturally be a matter for rejoicing, because the "lost are found." ❖

MESSAGE
—for—
TODAY

IT IS EASY to grow used to those whom we love most and forget to show appreciation for them. Perhaps the father in the parable had gotten too accustomed to living with his elder son or had not been able to show his love for him. It was only the catalyst of the younger son's return that enabled him to communicate how much he loved them both.

The point of the parable, however, is that God desires that all who have turned away from him will come back. The Gospel of Luke records Jesus as saying, "There will be more rejoicing in heaven over one sinner repenting than over 99 upright people who have no need of repentance [15:7]." To refuse God's love is like the prodigal son starving to death in a pigsty rather than returning to home and family.

A COMMITMENT *to* SEARCH

The LOST SHEEP ❖ *The* LOST COIN

LUKE 15:1–10; MATTHEW 18:12–14

❝ *Which one of you with a hundred sheep, if he lost one, would fail to leave the ninety-nine in the desert and go after the missing one till he found it?* ❞

LUKE 15:4

JESUS SEEMS TO have intended the parables of the Lost Sheep and the Lost Coin – as he did with that of the Prodigal Son (pp. 32–35) – to answer those who criticized him for preaching to the outcasts of society. In Luke's Gospel, Jesus told the parables in response to complaints of some of the scribes and Pharisees, that he welcomed and ate with sinners.

✝ *The Lost Sheep* ✝

Matthew places the parable of the Lost Sheep among a group of teachings about church discipline. It follows Jesus' warning that "the little ones" who have faith in Christ should not be led astray. Matthew seems to have been aiming this message at the leaders of the early church.

❖ In both Gospels, Jesus recounts the story of the Lost Sheep in the form of a question. Which man, he asked, if he owned 100 sheep, would not, if one were missing, leave the other 99 to go and look for it? In reality, it is unlikely that a Jewish sheep farmer would have left so many sheep untended in a desert (Luke) or on a hillside (Matthew). There is nothing in the texts to suggest that the sheep were in a fold or would have been looked after by a shepherd while the owner went to look for the missing one. Yet it was worth the risk of

A shepherd woman guides her flock of sheep across fields in Palestine. Jesus used the image of a shepherd even leaving the flock unattended to search for a lost sheep to convey the effort of God in looking for sinners.

leaving the flock unprotected, Jesus said, to recover the lost sheep.

In Matthew's account, the words "and if he find it" suggest an element of doubt about the outcome of the search. Luke, however, implies that the man would not give up the search until he found the missing sheep. He also says that when the man had located the lost sheep, he would joyfully carry it home – the conventional way would have been to put it on his shoulders, around his neck. Luke adds that the man would have invited his neighbors to rejoice with him over the sheep he had recovered – a detail that is reminiscent of the feast that was held to celebrate the return of the prodigal son.

† The Lost Coin †

With the second parable, Jesus again challenged his listeners to put themselves in the position of a person who had lost something. This time, the question supposed that a woman had lost a coin – one of her 10 drachmas. Would she not, Jesus asked, light a lamp and search her house until she found it? And having found it, would she not call together her friends and neighbors to celebrate with her?

Although a drachma was not a coin of much value, for a poor woman it would have been well worth the trouble of the search. It may also have been one of the coins used to adorn the headdress that women customarily wore as a sign of married status and so carried symbolic value.

In the dark peasant houses of the time, it would have been easy to lose a coin. However, the story's suggestion that the woman would invite people around to celebrate her finding it might seem farfetched.

The point of the story, as with the example of the Lost Sheep, is that just as men and women go to great lengths to recover a lost possession, so God will go to great trouble to win back just one of his lost children. This, Jesus suggested, should be a matter for rejoicing. ❖

MESSAGE
—for—
TODAY

IN THE MODERN Western world, people are more likely to fret about the loss of a key, a ring, or credit card than of a coin or a sheep. But a society in which people spend time and energy in recovering personal possessions does not always show the same determination to help those who are lost, such as the unemployed, the homeless, or alcoholics, to rediscover a meaningful worthwhile life.

People today may have trouble believing that God is so determined to find and bring home those who are separated from Him. When people accept God's love, however, they can pass it on with the same single-mindedness as the shepherd and the woman who lost the coin. This indeed is a cause for joyful celebration.

A GREATER SHOW
of LOVE

The TWO DEBTORS
LUKE 7:36–50

> ❝ *I tell you that her sins, many as they are, have been forgiven her, because she has shown such great love.* ❞
> #### LUKE 7:47

A SHORT, CLEAR STORY illustrating the generosity of God, the parable of the Two Debtors is memorable for the setting and circumstances in which Jesus told it. Some time during his ministry, Jesus dined with a Pharisee named Simon. As they ate and talked, a woman with a "bad name" attended to Jesus, washing and anointing his feet with oil. Simon was taken aback that Jesus should let such a woman touch him. So Jesus, in response to his reaction, told a parable about a man who was owed money by two men. One was due to repay him 500 denarii, the other 50. Neither man was able to pay his

A woman with a "bad name" uses her hair to wipe Jesus' feet while he dines with Simon the Pharisee, in this 15th-century Dutch painting.

debt, so the creditor let them both off. Which of the two, Jesus asked, would love the creditor more? Simon replied correctly that it was the one with the larger debt.

Jesus' parable in response to the action of the woman again sheds light on his attitude toward the religiously self-righteous – which some of the Pharisees apparently were – and the outcasts of society. While Simon respected Jesus enough to call him Rabbi, he did not receive him with the effusive warmth the woman had given him.

† The unknown woman †

It is not known who the woman was or whether she had met Jesus before. She may have come in when the doors were thrown open, along with beggars after tidbits of food, or with the admirers of a rabbi. This was customary at a Jewish banquet. Whoever she was, some scholars have suggested that she had already experienced the joy of forgiveness before meeting Jesus.

Others believe this joy followed her personal contact with him: so overwhelmed by meeting Jesus face to face was she that she had begun to weep. Her tears washed over Jesus' feet, and to wipe them away, she let her hair down – not an action a respectable woman would take in public. She then anointed his feet with myrrh.

Some scholars have pointed out that this parable may not be strictly analogous with the situation in which Jesus found himself when he told it. The message of the Two Debtors is that people will be generous with their love in proportion to their awareness of how much they have been forgiven. By contrast, the woman presumably showed her love for Jesus before he pronounced that her sins had been forgiven.

The link between the story and the woman's actions, however, may lie in Jesus' words, "It is someone who is forgiven little who shows little love." This oblique criticism of Simon suggests that outward piety with little love means far less than the abundant love of a repentant sinner. ❖

MESSAGE
—for—
TODAY

IT CAN BE DIFFICULT for people to break free of their past reputations. Ex-prisoners may find it hard to convince potential employers that they are reformed. People who have recovered from mental illness may still be viewed with suspicion by neighbors.

When a woman with a "bad name" approached Jesus, his host, Simon the Pharisee, judged her by her past. Jesus recognized in her openness and love the potential for change and a new life. He exemplified the divine ideal. It is important to be aware of any prejudices we may harbor toward others and react to these people according to the way they behave, not their reputation. If we are open to them, we may find that any prejudices they have toward us are also broken down, and in the process we may gain a clearer vision of our own need to be forgiven.

The PAYMENT of DEBTS

The UNFORGIVING SERVANT
MATTHEW 18:21–35

❝ *I canceled all that debt of yours when you appealed to me. Were you not bound, then, to have pity on your fellow servant just as I had pity on you?* ❞

MATTHEW 18:32–33

MATTHEW'S STORY of the Unforgiving Servant follows immediately an occasion when Peter questioned Jesus on how many times he should forgive his "brother if he wrongs me?" He asked whether seven times would be sufficient. Jesus replied, however, that he should forgive him not seven times, but seventy times seven. He then went on to illustrate the right attitude of forgiveness with a parable that conveys the overwhelming generosity of God.

Jesus told of a king who wanted to settle his accounts with his servants. The men were duly brought before him, and one of them was found to owe him the huge sum of 10,000 talents – a talent was a measurement that was used to weigh

The Roman denarius – shown here with the head of Emperor Tiberius (AD 14–37) – was one of the coins in circulation in Palestine at the time of Jesus. The coin was worth a laborer's work for one day.

money. The man did not have the means to pay. So the king ordered him to be sold, together with his wife, children, and all his possessions in order to get some compensation. But the servant threw himself at the king's feet and pleaded for time to repay the money. Taking pity on him, the king not only revoked the order to sell him and his family, but also canceled the whole debt.

† The second debtor †

No sooner had the man left the king's presence than he met a fellow servant who owed him 100 denarii. Unmoved by the fact that he had just had his own much larger debt wiped out, he violently grabbed the man and began to throttle him, demanding that he pay him all of the money. The debtor then fell to the ground and appealed for patience, just as the first servant had done a few minutes earlier in front of the king. But the forgiven man refused to listen and had the debtor thrown into prison until he could pay back the money.

Incensed by such cruelty, the other servants informed the king, who sent for the unforgiving servant. The King berated the man for his lack of pity and ordered him to be tortured, perhaps to force him to find friends or relations to pay his debts.

✝ God's generosity ✝

In this parable, Jesus compared the generosity of the king – that is, God – with the hard-hearted attitude of the servant. Jesus emphasized the generosity of God by stressing the huge amount the servant owed the king. The total annual income of Herod the Great, the Roman-backed ruler of Judea, has been estimated at about 900 talents: the servant in the story owed the king a staggering 10,000 talents.

> " And that is how
> my heavenly Father will deal
> with you unless you
> each forgive your brother
> from your heart. "
>
> MATTHEW 18:35

By contrast, the second servant's debt to the first of 100 denarii was still a substantial amount, but a drop in the ocean compared with the first debt. The king had acted with great compassion, despite the size of the sum owed, and canceled the debt. Lacking this compassion, the forgiven servant eventually received justice in place of the early mercy.

The story also points out that to be forgiven, a person must be able to forgive, a truth summed up by Jesus in his Sermon on the Mount (pp.64–71): "Yes, if you forgive others their failings, your heavenly Father will forgive you yours; but if you do not forgive others, your Father will not forgive your failings either [Matthew 6:14–15]." ❖

MESSAGE
—for—
TODAY

PEOPLE IN THE hot seat generally have a keen appreciation for forgiveness and mercy. Unfortunately, that attitude all too often changes when the person in trouble is someone else.

Jesus insisted that an awareness of personal weaknesses should make us more sympathetic toward other people's problems. Those who have experienced dark depths of despair to which humans can sink are often better equipped to help others in trouble. Reformed drug abusers, for example, are often the best counselors for young addicts wanting to break the habit. As "wounded healers," we can bring more comfort by sharing our weaknesses than by appearing strong. It is important to note that the servant was within his "rights" to respond to his debtor with justice – he undoubtedly had the law on his side. But to love as God does is to exercise mercy instead.

A WISE USE of MONEY

The CRAFTY STEWARD
LUKE 16:1–13

"The master praised the dishonest steward
for his astuteness. For the children
of this world are more astute in dealing with their own
kind than are the children of light."
LUKE 16:8

A NUMBER OF JESUS' parables concern the judgment of God after death. These stories warn that people must repent and be ready for this event, because it could happen at any time. Jesus' story of the Crafty Steward is one such admonition.

Jesus described the situation of a wealthy man – probably the owner of a large estate – whose steward was "wasteful" with his property. The rich man sent for his steward, asked for an account of his stewardship, then told the man that he was going to dismiss him: "Draw me up an account of your stewardship because you are not to be my steward any longer." Accordingly, the steward pondered how he was going to earn a living. He was too weak to

undertake manual work and too ashamed to beg. He decided to make sure that when he left his job, he would at least have some friends to help him out and give him hospitality. So he went to those who were in debt to his master and offered to alter their bonds and reduce their debts.

He told one man who owed 100 measures of oil to halve that amount, and told another to pay only 80 measures of wheat instead of 100. The story ends with the master praising the steward for his "astuteness."

Some commentators in recent times have argued that the

The Crafty Steward, at left, prepares for his dismissal by telling his master's debtors to reduce what they owed him, in this detail from a 19th-century British stained-glass window.

steward may not have been acting as dishonestly as the story suggests he was, because what he reduced from the debts was interest on the initial amount owed, and interest was forbidden by Jewish Law. In this case the steward would have been commended for setting matters right that he had handled dishonestly.

† Commending fraudulence? †

Other commentators believe that the story hinges on the man's apparent fraudulence and that Jesus intended to surprise his audience by appearing to praise his action. In fact, it is not clear whether the steward was commended by his employer or by Jesus. The Greek word *kyrios* means "master," but it also translates as "Lord" and is sometimes used by the Gospel writers to refer to Jesus.

If it was Jesus who praised the dishonest steward, it was not for his immoral behavior, but for his quick-thinking action to avert disaster. If a criminal prepares for dismissal with such thoroughness, Jesus seems to be suggesting, how much more urgently should people prepare themselves for the judgment of God?

In his Gospel, Luke follows the parable with a passage in which Jesus talked about the right way to use material wealth. Jesus said that although money in itself was "tainted," it could be put to good use — to make friends and, perhaps, to aid charities, acts that would earn the giver a reward in the next life.

Jesus ended the story with a warning that an excessive attachment to wealth would necessarily damage a person's relationship with God: "No servant can be the slave of two masters: he will either hate the first and love the second, or be attached to the first and despise the second. You cannot be the slave of God and money." In both this passage and the parable, Jesus suggested that although money may be an indispensable part of life, it should be used in a nonmaterialistic way, in the service of God and humanity. ❖

MESSAGE
—for—
TODAY

GOOD OR WELL-MEANING people are not always as smart or determined as those in the criminal underworld or, as in the parable, the crafty steward preparing for his dismissal. The Irish poet W. B. Yeats once wrote that "the best lack conviction, while the worst/Are filled with passionate intensity." The 18th-century British statesman Edmund Burke said, "It is necessary only for the good man to do nothing for evil to triumph."

Jesus insisted that his disciples should be as full of guile as serpents in their mission to spread the Gospel. Today, anyone fighting against injustice — whether it is the victimization of a colleague or the despoliation of a landscape by a multinational company — needs to show the same ingenuity as the steward. There is no virtue in pious naiveté when it subverts righteous action.

The SNARES of RICHES

The RICH FOOL ✤ The RICH MAN and LAZARUS

LUKE 12:16–21; 16:19–31.

❝ *Fool! This very night the demand will be made for your soul;
and this hoard of yours, whose will it be then?* ❞

LUKE 12:20

CONTAINING THE warning that judgment may come at any moment, the parables of the Rich Fool and of the Rich Man and Lazarus are also cautionary stories about the seductiveness of material wealth.

Jesus was alerting his listeners to the way in which wealth can make people feel self-reliant and self-satisfied. Content with a hedonistic life, they can easily neglect their spiritual selves and find themselves unprepared for death, which can come unexpectedly at any time.

✝ The Rich Fool ✝

Although in the Gospels, the Rich Fool is found only in Luke, a version of it appears in the Gospel of Thomas, an apocryphal text not included in the New Testament canon. In Luke, Jesus told the parable after a man in a crowd had asked Jesus to tell the man's brother to share his inheritance with him. Jesus replied that he was not a judge or an arbitrator of such claims and warned the man of the dangers of avarice. He then told the crowd a story.

There was a rich man, he said, who had reaped such an abundant harvest that he did not have enough space in his barns to store the crops. He decided, therefore, to pull down his barns to build bigger ones, telling his soul, "My soul, you have plenty of good things laid by for many years to come; take things easy, eat, drink, have a good time." But that very night, God warned him that he would die and would lose his hoarded wealth to someone else. This fate, Jesus added, lay in wait for anyone who stored up material, rather than spiritual, treasures.

✝ The Rich Man and Lazarus ✝

The story of the Rich Man – who is often known by his Latin name, Dives – and the beggar Lazarus is also a warning of judgment, as well as of the dangers of selfish misuse of money. The rich man, Jesus said, lived a life of luxury, dressing in purple and fine linen and feasting every day. Since the story implies that he and his brothers had no belief in the afterlife, he was probably understood to be one of the Sadducees – aristocratic Jews who were associated with the Temple administration, who did not believe in life after death. This attitude toward death may have influenced the man's selfish lifestyle and his lack of compassion for those in need.

Lazarus is the only character whom Jesus actually names in his parables. This may be because his name, which means "God helps," emphasizes the role he plays in the story. Jesus

The rich man ignores Lazarus, who starves at his gate, while enjoying a feast, in this medieval Bulgarian mural. In the afterlife, their respective fortunes are reversed.

ЛАЗАР

ПРИТЧА ЗА БОГА́ТАГО
И НИ́ЩАГО ЛАЗАРА

described him as a cripple, covered with sores, who longed to eat the scraps from Dives's feasts. At Jewish banquets, guests would often wipe their hands on pieces of bread that they then threw on the floor. After the meal, these scraps were usually given to the hungry. But Dives was too selfish, it seems, to allow even this sharing of wealth. In the meantime, Lazarus lay starving at his gate while the dogs licked his sores.

Both Lazarus and the rich man then died. Lazarus was taken by the angels into the arms of the great Jewish Patriarch Abraham – that is, heaven. The rich man was sent to Hades, or hell, where he saw Abraham and Lazarus in the distance, across the great gulf that divided them. In torment from the flames of Hades, Dives begged Abraham to send Lazarus to dip the tip of his finger in water and cool his tongue. But Abraham refused his plea, pointing out that he had enjoyed luxury on Earth while Lazarus had suffered much. Now, in the afterlife, their roles were reversed.

The rich man asked Abraham to send Lazarus back to Earth to warn his brothers so that they

In the story of Si-Osiris, the poor on Earth enjoy the blessings of the afterlife, shown as abundant fields of wheat and fruit trees in this Egyptian tomb mural.

could avoid hell's torments. Again, Abraham refused: "They have Moses and the prophets, let them listen to them." Dives insisted that if someone came to his brothers from the dead, they would definitely take notice and repent. Abraham retorted that if they would not listen to Moses and the prophets, a messenger from the dead would not make any difference at all.

+ The Egyptian underworld +

For the first part of the parable, Jesus seems to have been drawing on a Jewish folktale that was itself derived from an Egyptian story. In this, a character named Si-Osiris conducted his father to the underworld in order to show him the respective fates of the rich and the poor in the afterlife. The story ends with the words, "He who has been good on Earth will be blessed in the kingdom of the dead, and he who has been evil on Earth will suffer in the kingdom of the dead."

> **" Lazarus... longed to fill himself with what fell from the rich man's table. "**
>
> LUKE 16:21

Jesus' parable contains a similar message. Dives stood condemned because his wealth had diverted him from a sense of compassion for Lazarus. That he had, during his lifetime, been aware of the existence of Lazarus and the nature of his plight is shown by the fact that he recognized him in the afterlife. In addition, by saying that the rich man's brothers had ignored Moses and the prophets, Jesus implicated his Jewish opponents, whom he accused of doing the same thing.

Certainly, the assertion that the brothers would not be convinced "even if someone should rise from the dead" would have struck a chord with early Christians, who were acutely conscious of the fact that most contemporary Jews had refused to believe in the resurrection of Jesus. ❖

MESSAGE —for— TODAY

WEALTH, JESUS suggested, should be a means to an end, never an end in itself. Furthermore, the end should not be guided by selfishness, but by a desire to help others.

People who have more money than they need for their immediate requirements carry the responsibility of using it wisely, not wastefully. A traditional Jewish saying states that the rich help the poor in this world, but the poor help the rich in the afterlife. No matter how many insurance policies are taken out, wealth cannot provide ultimate security or protection from mortality. But it can be used to foster relationships and alleviate poverty. Spiritual, lasting wealth has nothing to do with money and belongings, which can come and go with the flick of a flame or the crash of a wave.

BEARING FRUIT

The TRUE VINE ❖ *The* BARREN FIG TREE

JOHN 15:1–17; LUKE 13:1–9

> ❝ *I am the vine, you are the branches.*
> *Whoever remains in me, with me*
> *in him, bears fruit in plenty; for cut off*
> *from me you can do nothing.* ❞
>
> JOHN 15:5

THE TRUE VINE and the Barren Fig Tree are two parables that use imagery drawn from trees and horticulture, and both indicate that those who do not produce spiritual fruit face destruction, unless they repent.

✝ *The True Vine* ✝

During the Last Supper, described in a passage in John's Gospel, Jesus compared himself to a vine and warned his listeners that those who did not bear fruit would be destroyed. Jesus described the indissoluble relationship between God, himself, and his disciples in terms of viticulture. God, the Father, was the vinedresser, Jesus was the true vine, and the disciples were the branches. If the disciples remained in Jesus, they would bear fruit. If not, they would wither and be cast into the fire. He went on to say that the binding force between them was love. He had loved his disciples as his Father had loved him, and he had chosen them to "go out and bear fruit, fruit that will last." The passage ends with Jesus saying, "My command to you is to love one another."

Like the fig tree, the vine was also used in the Old Testament to symbolize Israel. In a passage in the book of Isaiah, for example, God speaks of his care for his vineyard – Israel. The metaphor

ends with a warning of destruction: "Why, when I expected it to yield fine grapes, has it yielded wild ones?...I shall let it go to waste, unpruned, undug...[5:4–6]." John's assertion that Jesus is the true vine is therefore a claim that the church is the true Israel. Those who abide in Jesus are the people of God; those who do not will be thrown away and burned.

Jesus was addressing his disciples and warning them against unfaithfulness. It was essential, he said, that they should remain in him, even though they might encounter pressures to abandon their faith in him and their obedience to the way of life he had taught them. They had to grasp that they could do nothing apart from him – an idea he emphasized by saying he was not just the stem of the vine but the whole vine, of which the branches – the disciples – were part.

In a similar way, Saint Paul, in his first letter to the church at Corinth, compared the church of Christ to a whole body, whose parts could not be separated from Jesus Christ: "For as with the human body, which is a unity although it has many parts – all the parts of the body, though

Vines were a common sight in Palestine in the time of Jesus – just as they are today. Jesus used the image of the vine to illustrate the unity between the disciples (the branches) and himself (the whole vine).

many, still making up one single body – so it is with Christ… if the whole body were just an eye, how would there be hearing? [12:12–17]." Jesus promised that if his disciples remained in him and his words remained in them, they would bear much fruit and glorify the Father.

✝ The Barren Fig Tree ✝

The second parable tells of a man who had planted a fig tree in his vineyard. For three years he came to look for fruit on the tree, but found none. So he told his vinedresser to cut it down, because it was a waste of space. The story ends with the vinedresser pleading that the tree be given one more year. During this time, he would dig around it and fertilize it, and if it still did not bear any fruit, then it should be cut down.

The story of the fig tree follows and is related to a passage in Luke that alludes to an atrocity committed by Pontius Pilate, the Roman prefect of Judea. Pilate had apparently killed several Galileans while they were offering sacrifices at the Temple. Referring to the dead Galileans, as well as to 18 people who had been accidentally killed by a collapsing tower in Jerusalem, Jesus said that none of them had been killed because of any particular sin. The victims were no more guilty than anyone else in the city. Everyone would suffer punishment unless they repented. The important point that Jesus

Fig trees were commonly grown in Palestine at the time of Jesus. He used the image of a barren fig tree to illustrate the fact that his mission to the Jews had not been successful.

was trying to make was that the death of others should cause the living to consider their own spiritual condition. He then illustrated this need for repenting – and the dire consequence of not doing so – with the story of the fig tree.

> ❝ *'Sir,' the man replied, 'leave it one more year and give me time to dig round it and manure it: it may bear fruit next year; if not, then you can cut it down.'* ❞
> LUKE 13:8–9

In ancient Palestine, it was not unusual for fig trees to be planted in vineyards because there was little other fertile land. Fig trees absorb a lot of moisture and nourishment, so the one in the story would have needed to have borne fruit to justify its place in the vineyard.

According to Jewish Law (Leviticus 19:23), the first three years of a fig tree's growth were allowed to elapse before the fruit was deemed ritually clean. If the vineyard owner had looked for fruit for three years, the tree would have been already six years old and hopelessly barren. The message of the story is that the tree is given one more opportunity. The fig tree is often used to symbolize Israel in the Old Testament, as Jesus seems to have used it in this parable, indicating that his call to the

A vine grows out of a pot, in this AD sixth-century Byzantine mosaic. Vines were often depicted in Christian art and were used to symbolize Jesus as the "true vine."

Jews to repent had not borne fruit. Yet, they still had a last chance to respond. Some scholars have also speculated that the three years during which the owner looked for fruit could signify the period of Jesus' ministry.

Although only Luke relates this parable in his Gospel, both Mark and Matthew tell of an occasion during Jesus' last week in Jerusalem before his death when he cursed a fig tree outside the city for not bearing fruit – an incident that Luke does not include. Some scholars, therefore, believe that the story of the cursing may have originated as a parable, a version of which appeared in Luke's Gospel. Certainly, unlike the tree in the parable, the cursed fig tree was not given a second chance. Perhaps by that stage of his ministry, just a few days before his crucifixion, Jesus wanted to illustrate that the opportunity to repent had been missed. ❖

MESSAGE
for
TODAY

RELIGION IS NOT simply a matter of going to church and performing the appropriate rituals. It is about being connected to God in such a way that loving acts and words of kindness can blossom from the source of life.

In both of these parables, Jesus spoke of the importance of bearing spiritual fruit. In his image of the vine, he stressed the closeness of the relationship that would produce spiritual behavior: only through a resolve to work through the power of God can people tap into the divine source of energy. In the story of the fig tree, Jesus warned that people cannot delay changing their lives indefinitely. He stressed that those who have been made aware of a new spiritual way of living must show it in their lives. If they do not, the consequences may be drastic. They will get what they have explicitly, or by implication, asked for – separation from God.

Obeying God's Will

The Two Sons ❖ The Wicked Husbandmen

MARK 12:1–12; MATTHEW 21:28–46;
LUKE 20:9–19

> ❝ *Jesus said to them, 'In truth I tell you,*
> *tax collectors and prostitutes are*
> *making their way into the kingdom*
> *of God before you.'* ❞
> MATTHEW 21:31

JESUS TOLD THE parable of the Two Sons, recorded only by Matthew, and the story of the Wicked Husbandmen, which occurs in all three Synoptic Gospels, at a critical moment in his ministry. Shortly before, he had entered Jerusalem in triumph on a donkey, much to the rejoicing of his followers.

Inside the city, he had then gone to the Temple, where he threw out those who were buying and selling goods and changing money, making it, in Jesus' words, "a den of thieves." While he was there, blind and lame people came to him and he healed them.

When he returned to the Temple the next day to teach, the chief priests challenged him to state what authority he had for his actions. But Jesus retorted that he would answer their question only if they first replied to his: referring to his cousin, John the Baptist – regarded by the church as the forerunner of Jesus – he asked them whether John's authority had come from a divine or human source. They declined to answer.

Because those who had acknowledged John the Baptist as a messenger of God would also have seen the spiritual status of Jesus, it is not surprising that Jesus' opponents were loath to admit to the divine source of John's authority. On the other hand, they knew that if they denied that the Baptist had authority from God, they risked offending the people, who regarded him as a prophet. So, since his question had not elicited a reply from the priests, Jesus also refused to answer their probings about his own authority. Instead, he told them a parable.

✝ The Two Sons ✝

There was a man, Jesus said, who had two sons. He asked the first to go and work in his vineyard, but the son refused. Later, however, he changed his mind and went to work. When the other son was approached, he agreed to go, but in fact did not do so. Jesus then asked his audience, "Which of the two did the father's will?" His listeners answered that it was the first son, who had actually carried out the work his father had requested him to do.

Jesus made the story's application clear – that "sinners" were entering the kingdom in the place of Jews who regarded themselves as pious: "For John came to you, showing the way of uprightness, but you did not believe him, and yet the tax collectors and prostitutes did."

Mark (11:27–33) and Luke (20:1–8) also recount the incident in the Temple when the

chief priests, as well as the scribes and "elders," challenged Jesus' authority for his actions. But they do not retell this parable. On the one hand, Matthew seems to have placed it here to show Jesus reinforcing his assertion that the Jews' religious leaders, despite their professed obedience to the will of God, were actually disobedient to it. On the other hand, those

❖ *Two of the wicked husbandmen mortally wound one of the vineyard owner's servants, in this detail from a 14th-century German altarpiece.*

generally despised by society, such as the tax collectors and prostitutes, had repented and turned to God in response to the preaching of John the Baptist.

† The Wicked Husbandmen †

The parable of the Wicked Husbandmen, like John's comparison of Jesus to the true vine (pp. 48–50), uses the vineyard to symbolize Israel, a traditional identification found in the Old Testament. The story is about a householder who

Palestinian laborers pick grapes in a vineyard. In Jesus' allegorical parable, the tenants' abusive treatment of the householder's servants caused their own destruction and loss of land.

planted a vineyard, placed a fence around it, dug a winepress, and built a tower. He then rented it to vine growers (husbandmen) and went abroad. When it was time for the vines to bear fruit, he sent a servant (Matthew says servants) to collect his share of the rent. The tenants, however, instead of honoring their agreement, beat the servant and sent him away empty-handed. When a second man was sent, the tenants also physically abused him.

According to Luke's account, a third servant was wounded; according to Mark, who also mentions that additional servants were sent, the servants were killed. This may be echoing Old Testament references to the many prophets whom the Jews had repudiated and martyred (1 Kings 18:13; 2 Chronicles 24:20 ff).

> **❝ *This is the heir. Come on, let us kill him and take over his inheritance.' So they seized him and threw him out of the vineyard and killed him.* ❞**
> MATTHEW 21:38–39

The landowner then decided to send his son – Mark calls him his "beloved son," which was the phrase used by the voice from heaven to address Jesus at his baptism in the Jordan: "You are my Son, the Beloved; my favor rests on you [1:11]." The owner had hoped that even if the tenants had treated his servants badly, they would at least respect his son. Instead, egging each other on to kill him and inherit the property, they threw him out of the vineyard and murdered him.

Jesus asked what the owner of the vineyard would do, then answered his own question by saying that he would destroy the tenants and give the vineyard to others. The audience, according to Luke, reacted to this drastic action with the words, "God forbid!" Quoting from the Psalms (118:22–23), Jesus responded by alluding to his own rejection by the Jews and the founding of the church. He ended by saying that the kingdom of God would be given to those who bore fruit.

✝ The True Israel ✝

The meaning of the parable lies in its allegorical details. The tenants stand for Israel's rulers and leaders, the owner of the vineyard is God, the messengers are the prophets, the son is Christ, and the punishment symbolizes the destruction of Israel.

The "others," to whom the vineyard is given, probably refers to the Gentiles, who made up the majority of the church, claimed by its members to be the True Israel. Early Christians may also have seen the son being cast out of the vineyard as picturing the fact that Jesus was crucified outside the walls of Jerusalem.

The incident concludes with the scribes and priests wanting to arrest Jesus, but being afraid to do so because they feared the reaction of the people. From this, it is clear that Jesus had strong popular support – it was presumably to avoid a public outcry that the authorities later decided to arrest Jesus at night.

Some Jews may have wanted Jesus put to death, while others clearly supported him. On his way to his death by crucifixion, for example, the women of Jerusalem wept for him (Luke 23:28). The early Christians, however, perhaps influenced by the growing hostility between the church and the synagogue, tended to blame all Jews for the death of Jesus. Many of them accused the Jewish people of deicide, killing God, an idea that has now been repudiated by almost all churches.

Jesus' parable, with its explicit reference to the death of the son, could have alerted Jesus' followers to the fate that was in store for him. At the same time, Jesus may have intended it to be a final appeal to his opponents to consider the consequences of their actions. ❖

MESSAGE
—for—
TODAY

JESUS IMPLIED that the violence with which the tenants treated the landlord's servants had occurred in the past with Israel's rejection of God's prophets. For the early Christians, however, the story also reflected their own persecution at the hands of the Roman authorities. Many who suffered martyrdom were sustained until the end by the conviction that God's kingdom of justice would eventually come.

In the 20th century, persecution fueled by an intolerance of others' beliefs, nationality, or race has continued unabated. The right to speak, publish, or worship without fear of persecution is worth fighting for in any society, even if we do not agree with or relate to others' opinions or religious rituals. Jesus encouraged people to remain true to their convictions. Strength to do so in the face of intolerance comes from faith in a just and merciful God.

An INVITATION to the FEAST

The GREAT BANQUET ❖
The WEDDING FEAST

MATTHEW 22:1–14; LUKE 14:16–24

*" Go to the main crossroads and invite everyone
you can find to come to the wedding. "*

MATTHEW 22:8

T HE GOSPELS OF Matthew and Luke both include similar parables about an important feast to which those invited made various excuses and did not come. Both stories warn of the perils of refusing Jesus' invitation to enter the kingdom of God. Luke's parable tells of a man who arranged a great banquet to which he invited many guests. At the time of the meal, he sent his servants to ❖ tell the guests that everything was ready. But the guests began to make excuses. One said he had to attend to a piece of land he had just bought; another wanted to try out five new yoke of oxen; and a third said he had just married.

Men, women and children prepare for the wedding feast of the king's son, in this depiction of the event painted by the 16th-century French school of Martin de Vos.

In ancient Palestine, the usual time for business exchanges was in the early evening, after the main work of the day had ended. So the guests may have intended to come to the banquet later. According to contemporary etiquette, people could arrive late to a formal meal, provided they came before the end of the first course.

In any case, the host was furious at his guests' attitude and sent a servant out to invite people who were poor, crippled, blind, and lame. After the servant had carried out the host's orders, he reported that there was still room for more people. So the master ordered him to go out and bring in people from the neighboring countryside.

Jesus' story clearly contrasts the indifference and hostility of the religious leaders – the invited guests – and the outcasts of society, who flocked to hear Jesus preach. It also implies that the invitation of Jesus originated from God: those who refused to repent and believe would find no place in the kingdom of God.

✝ The Wedding Feast ✝

In Matthew's story, a king who was holding a marriage feast for his son sent out messengers to tell the guests to come to the celebrations. Not only did the guests give excuses, but some of them also seized and killed the messengers. In revenge, the king destroyed the murderers and burned their town.

The great banquet was a traditional image of the messianic feast that Jews believed would inaugurate the new world order ushered in by the Messiah. In the parable, Jesus insisted that no one had an automatic right to a place in the Kingdom, only those who responded to God's call.

Jesus ended the parable by telling of a guest who was not wearing a wedding garment. As a result, the king had him bound and thrown out into the darkness outside. The point of the parable is that people must be properly dressed – that is, spiritually prepared – before they enter into God's Kingdom. ❖

MESSAGE —for— TODAY

MOMENTS OR SITUATIONS that can affect or change people's lives often come out of the blue. They may appear in the form of job offer or a proposal of marriage. Or there may be a moment of clarity in which we see in ourselves the need to reform or be forgiven. It may be tempting to make excuses and turn down opportunities that suddenly present themselves. We may feel too insecure about our ability to rise to the challenge or not want to disturb our daily routines. Certainly the invited guests turned down a unique invitation to attend to practical matters that could have waited until the day after.

People rarely regret having seized a challenge. At the very least, they test themselves, and can take pride from the fact that they had the courage to take it on in the first place. At the same time, they may discover that the challenge was indeed a call from God.

The BRIDEGROOM'S ARRIVAL

The TEN WEDDING ATTENDANTS
MATTHEW 25:1–13

❝ But at midnight there was a cry, 'Look!
The bridegroom! Go out and meet him.' ❞
MATTHEW 25:6

D URING A DISCOURSE with his disciples on the Mount of Olives outside Jerusalem, Jesus prophesied how the end of the world would come about. Then, to stress the need to be ready for this moment and his Second Coming – when he would return after his death and resurrection to usher in the end of the world – he told a story about ten wedding attendants, traditionally known as the "wise and foolish virgins."

Locked out of the wedding hall, the foolish attendants appeal in vain to be allowed to enter, in this painting by the 16th-century Italian artist Tintoretto.

These women, Jesus said, set out with their oil lamps to meet a bridegroom, presumably to escort him to the bride's home for the wedding, as was the custom. Five of them took flasks of oil to replenish their lamps, but five "foolish" ones did not. The bridegroom was delayed, however, and the attendants became drowsy and fell asleep. Not until midnight were they roused by a shout, warning them that he was now approaching.

To their horror, the five "foolish" attendants found that their lamps were going out. They asked the others to share their oil, but the wise attendants refused, fearing that if they did so their own lamps might also run out of oil before the wedding procession reached the bride's house. So the foolish attendants went off to buy more oil. By the time they returned, the bridegroom and the other attendants had already entered the wedding hall, and the door was locked. When they called out for the door to be opened, they received the chilling reply, "In truth I tell you I do not know you," which really means in effect, "I don't want to have anything to do with you."

† The need for vigilance †

Jesus seems originally to have intended the story to carry a warning to his hearers – be aware that the kingdom of God is at hand and seize the moment of salvation by being ready for the arrival of the bridegroom, a figure Jesus identified with himself elsewhere (Mark 2:19).

But after Jesus' death and resurrection, the early church saw the parable as a warning to be alert and ready for Jesus' Second Coming. Even if, like the bridegroom in the parable, Jesus' return was delayed, Christians should "stay awake for you do not know either the day or the hour." Some later manuscripts make clearer the reference of the return of the Son of man. Christians, the parable teaches, must be prepared at all times: it is crucial not to leave spiritual readiness to the last moment, for then it may be too late. ❖

MESSAGE
—for—
TODAY

JESUS WARNED his followers that they should prepare themselves for the arrival of the kingdom of God. The story of the wedding attendants is a cautionary tale against missing out on a unique opportunity.

It is important to keep in a state of readiness for any challenging situation life might have in store for us. When Sir Winston Churchill became prime minister of Great Britain during World War II, he declared that his whole life had been a preparation for leading his country at one of the darkest moments in its history.

Just so, Jesus taught, should people of faith view the life they are given to live. Being in a state of readiness may in itself present new openings, situations, or guidance. Even more, as an ancient Chinese proverb says, "When the student is ready, the master will come."

A SPIRITUAL INVESTMENT

The TALENTS ❖ The POUNDS

MATTHEW 25:14–30; LUKE 19:12–27

❝ Well done, good and trustworthy servant…come and join your master's happiness. ❞

MATTHEW 25:21

SEVERAL WARNINGS about the danger of not fulfilling spiritual potential appear in the Gospel accounts of Jesus' ministry. The parable of the Talents – using a unit of weight measurement applied to money to symbolize spiritual gifts – and the similar story of the Pounds are found in the Gospels of Matthew and Luke. Another version also appears in the apocryphal Gospel of the Hebrews, or Nazarenes, which was used by Jewish Christians living in Syria during the fourth century.

† The Talents †

In all three accounts, servants were entrusted with money by their master before he traveled to a distant country. In Matthew and Luke, two servants used their bequest to make more money, while a third buried what he was given in the ground. In the Gospel of the Hebrews, one servant multiplied his money, one buried it, and the third spent it on harlots.

In Matthew's version, when the master returned and called his servants to account, he praised the two who had doubled the talents he had given them. But he berated the third, who

These silver shekels and the bronze pot, found in Palestine, date from the AD first century. Jesus used the image of hoarding coins – as opposed to investing them – to illustrate the danger of not developing spiritually.

had buried his money, calling him wicked and lazy and telling him that he should at least have placed it in a bank so that interest could have accrued. He then had this man's money confiscated and gave it to the first servant.

Matthew intended the story as a warning to the faithful. Just as the master came back expecting his servants to have used his money profitably, so Jesus, when he returned in judgment as the Son of man after his death and resurrection, would expect his servants to have developed their spiritual gifts. It is a theme that is continued with the parable of the Sheep and the Goats (pp. 62–63), which Matthew tells after this story.

✝ The Pounds ✝

Luke's version of the parable tells of a nobleman who went to a far country – one that apparently had control over his country – seeking to be endorsed as king over his own people. Before leaving, he gave money to ten of his servants, telling them to trade with it. On his return, the nobleman, now a king, rewarded two servants for increasing the money. But he censured a third for keeping it safe and not investing it.

Luke's story contains details that appear to reflect a real historical circumstance. While the king was abroad, one of his compatriots, who detested him, sent a delegation to the foreign power to protest against his appointment. This is, in fact, what happened in 4 BC. After the death of Herod the Great – the Roman-backed king of Judea – his son Archelaus journeyed to Rome to be invested as the new king. A Jewish embassy of 50 people also traveled to Rome in order to resist his appointment.

When he returned – as king – Archelaus inflicted a bloody revenge upon his people. Later generations did not forget, and the memory of it may be reflected in the parable's last verse: "As for my enemies…bring them here and execute them in my presence." ❖

MESSAGE
—for—
TODAY

THE WORD GIFTED is usually applied to those noted for their creative, sporting, or professional ability. Gifted athletes, actors, and writers often seem to have more than their fair share of God's gifts. A gift, however, may consist of something less glamorous, but just as valid and necessary for self, community, and even humankind. Teaching, nursing, raising children, listening to others' problems – all these require different but equally valid gifts.

Jesus did not indicate a pecking order of spiritual gifts. However, he did insist that whatever gifts people have been given, they should not "bury them in the ground" – that is, waste, hide, or ignore them. What is important is to identify one's abilities, no matter how humble they seem, and to fulfill their potential in faith that in the gifts lie life's greatest joy and contribution.

The FINAL SEPARATION

The SHEEP and the GOATS
MATTHEW 25:31–46

❝ When did we see you a stranger and make
you welcome, lacking clothes and
clothe you?... And the King will answer,
'In truth I tell you, in so far as you did this to one
of the least of these brothers of mine,
you did it to me.' ❞

MATTHEW 25:38–40

THE LAST PARABLE that Matthew records in his Gospel is about the Last Judgment, when Jesus – referred to in the story as both the Son of man and the King – will judge people on the way they have conducted their lives. The contrast drawn between those who live faithfully and those who do not is a recurring theme in Jesus' parables, and here it is clear that the expected fruit of faith is a compassionate concern for those who are in need.

Addressing his disciples, Jesus began by saying that the Son of man would come in glory, escorted by "all the angels," to judge "all nations" that would be assembled before him. "Son of man" is an enigmatic term often used in the Gospels to describe Jesus, and here Matthew connects it to both the suffering that awaited him and the promise that he would return. The reference to the nations shows that Jesus' concern was not just with the fate of the Jews, but of the Gentiles as well.

The Son of man, Jesus said, would separate the people assembled before him, placing some on his right side and others on his left. Jesus likened this process to the separation of sheep from goats that a Palestinian shepherd would carry out every evening, because goats needed to be kept warm at night, while sheep preferred the open air.

✝ Entry into God's kingdom ✝

The King, Jesus continued, would then address those on his right and invite them into God's kingdom: "Come, you whom my father has blessed, take as your heritage the kingdom prepared for you since the foundation of the world." He explained that when he was thirsty, hungry, sick, lacked clothes, or was in prison, they had responded to his needs.

Puzzled by this assertion, the people would ask when they had seen him in these different states of wretchedness. He would answer that in attending to the wants of the most wretched person, they had attended to his. Then the King would turn to those on his left and consign them to "eternal fire," because they had failed to do what the compassionate had done: "Go away from me, with your curse upon you, to the eternal fire for the devil and his angels."

Some biblical commentators have pointed out that the people in the story seem to be judged

according to their deeds, rather than their belief in God. In the parable of the Rich Man and Lazarus (pp. 44–47), however, Jesus made it clear that it was the rich man's lack of belief in God that had been the cause of his uncharitable attitude toward Lazarus.

The parable also addresses the question about the fate of the Gentiles at the Last Judgment, which was a subject of debate among contemporary Jews. Some believed that at the end of time, Gentiles would turn from their idolatry and obey God. This idea was developed during

Flanked by two angels, Jesus separates the sheep from the goats, in this sixth-century Byzantine mosaic. The sheep, on his right, represent those who have earned an invitation to the kingdom of God, whereas the goats symbolize the sinners who are damned.

the AD first century, and some Jewish teachers, such as a certain Rabbi Joshua, held the view that all those who had been righteous during their lives on earth – no matter whether they were Gentiles or Jews – would inherit a share in the life of the world to come.

In the early church, there were heated debates about whether Gentiles who came to faith in Jesus had to convert first to Judaism, as many "God-fearers" – Gentiles who were attracted to the monotheism and high ethical teaching of Judaism – responded to Paul's preaching of the Gospel.

✝ True believers ✝

The church eventually decided that this conversion was not required. The book of Acts relates how James told his fellow apostles and elders that it was wrong to make things "more difficult for Gentiles who turn to God [15:19]."

Reflecting this spirit of toleration, Matthew probably intended this parable to sum up one of the themes of his Gospel: that true believers in the Son of man, whether they are Jews or Gentiles, are those who bring forth good fruit and show acts of mercy (9:13; 12:7). ❖

A modern-day Palestinian shepherd tends his flock of sheep. The traditional practice of separating sheep and goats was used by Jesus to illustrate the way the blessed and the sinners would be divided at the Last Judgment.

MESSAGE
—for—
TODAY

IN HIS DESCRIPTION of the Last Judgment, Jesus identified himself with the most wretched members of society and made clear that what was done for those in greatest need was done for Jesus himself. The New Testament letter of James reiterates the point: "Pure, unspoiled religion … is this: coming to the help of orphans and widows in their hardships … [1:27]."

In the Greek Orthodox church, there is a tradition that people should never refuse hospitality to any stranger because that person might be Jesus. Similarly, the Indian statesman Mahatma Gandhi once said, "If you don't find God in the very next person you meet, it is a waste of time looking for him further." Helping the needy is an act not only of human compassion, but also of religious faith. The commandments to love God and to love our neighbor are inseparable.

THE SERMONS OF JESUS

BOTH MATTHEW'S and John's Gospels record a number of sermons or discourses that Jesus related privately to his disciples or in public to a crowd of people. Although they are supposed to have been uttered by Jesus on specific occasions, it is likely that some contain sayings that Jesus spoke at various times, which were later collected and presented as unified sermons.

Some scholars have suggested that Matthew's Gospel falls into five sections – plus an account of Jesus' passion and resurrection – and that each of those sections ends with a sermon or discourse. Two of these are the Sermon on the Mount (pp. 66–71) and the sermon about the Last Judgment (pp. 76–78). In the Sermon on the Mount – the core of Jesus' teaching about the Christian life – Matthew portrays Jesus as the new Moses, who has come not to "abolish" Jewish religious traditions, but to complete them. And, in his vivid warnings about the end of the world and the Last Judgment, Jesus prophesied the destruction of Jerusalem and how he would return, as the Son of man, on the clouds of heaven.

In John's Gospel, Jesus' sermons tend to be more reflective, and several of them include sayings that begin "I am" – a phrase that echoes God's revelation to Moses (Exodus 3:14). In addressing a crowd at Capernaum (pp. 72–75), for example, Jesus told them that he was the "bread of life" and continued to use imagery of bread to illustrate the relationship among himself, the believer, and God. ❖

The NEW WAY of LIVING

The SERMON on the MOUNT
MATTHEW 5–7

**❝ *Blessed are the pure in heart:*
they shall see God. ❞**

MATTHEW 5:8

FORMING THE HEART of Jesus' teaching, the Sermon on the Mount contains some of his most evocative sayings and images. Matthew suggests that Jesus delivered the sermon to his disciples on one particular occasion, addressing them from a hillside. The sermon appears, not surprisingly, also to represent a collection of Jesus' teachings that he uttered on various occasions. Although the sermon is best known from Matthew, many of its parts appear at different places in Luke's Gospel as well.

Intended by Matthew to be viewed as a new development of the Jewish Law, or Torah – the basis of which God revealed to Moses on Mount Sinai (Exodus 20) – the sermon can be divided into five sections. The first consists of the Beatitudes – eight pronouncements describing the rewards of those who act or suffer in the name of Jesus. In the second, Jesus contrasts the new righteousness of his teaching with the requirements of the Jewish Law. The third section describes the appropriate expressions of piety, such as almsgiving, prayer, and fasting. The fourth encourages complete trust in God's care. And finally, Jesus tells a story about a wise and a foolish man to describe the nature of true discipleship, that is, faithfully following Jesus.

The Beatitudes take their name from the Latin *beatus*, "blessed." Jesus' first beatitude commends those who are "poor in spirit" (Luke simply says "poor"), which is a term used in the Old Testament to refer to the pious (Psalm 35:10). In the two centuries before Jesus, the term was virtually a synonym for the Hasid, the saintly or pious of Israel. The reward of the pious, Jesus was saying, was to enter the kingdom of Heaven.

✝ The gentle and pure in heart ✝

Jesus then said that those who were gentle would inherit the earth, and those who mourned would be comforted. Those who hungered and thirsted for "uprightness" would have their prayers answered, while the merciful would receive mercy. The reward for the "pure in heart" is described as seeing God.

The peacemakers, Jesus continued, would be recognized as "children of God." The price of peacemaking and living a holy life was often persecution, as the Christians who read Matthew's Gospel knew to their cost; and Jesus addressed his final beatitude to those persecuted in the cause of "uprightness." Their reward – that "the kingdom of Heaven is theirs" – meant that they would come into the presence of God; "heaven" was often used by pious Jews as a substitute for God's sacred name.

Following this theme of persecution, Jesus encouraged his disciples not to lose faith for fear of opposition. He told them that they were "salt for the earth," and if salt lost its taste it was useless: just as salt played a useful part in cooking, preserving, and "healing," so the faithful served, by their

sacrifice and intercession, to turn humankind to God. Jesus went on to say that his disciples were the light of the world, and they and their good works should shine for all to see – in the way that a hilltop city is revealed to everyone or a lamp on a lampstand provides light for the whole house.

After enjoining his disciples to remain faithful, Jesus said that he had not come to abolish the "Law or Prophets" – that is, the legal and

Jesus sets out his teachings to an expectant crowd, in this painting of the Sermon on the Mount by the 16th-century Flemish painter Joos de Momper.

religious traditions of the Jews – but to complete them. Biblical scholars have debated exactly what Jesus meant by his statement that he had not come to abolish the Law. Some Christians, partly influenced by the letters of Saint Paul, have felt that Jews could earn God's favor only by obeying every letter of the Law with joyless rigor. But, by and large, Jews regarded the Law as a God-given gift and a privilege.

† Fulfilling the Law †

Many Christian scholars, taking their lead from Jesus' criticism of some of the Pharisees' attitudes, think that Jesus' apparent loyalty to the Law is surprising. But a growing number of scholars now regard Jesus as a pious Jew who dutifully kept the Law: Jesus was not undermining it, but completing it, by calling for more radical and inward obedience to God.

> " *Do not imagine that I have come to abolish the Law or Prophets.* "
>
> MATTHEW 5:17

In the rest of the fifth chapter, Matthew relates how Jesus spelled out the difference between inward and outward obedience. Referring to the injunction in the Ten Commandments not to kill, Jesus said that even harboring anger would be answerable before a local court. Furthermore, calling your brother a fool, he said, was as bad as murder and would result in an appearance in the Sanhedrin, the supreme court of the Jews. Calling him a traitor was an even more grievous offense, punishable by hellfire.

Jesus then insisted that making an offering at the Temple in Jerusalem was pointless if any outstanding arguments had not been settled first. He declared that disputes should be settled quickly before they escalated and led to more trouble. He went on to say that if a man looked at a woman lustfully, he had already committed adultery with her in his heart. Rather than give in to temptation, it was better for people to tear out their right eye and cut off their right hand and so prevent the whole of their body from

Oil lamps similar to this Roman one were used in Palestinian houses in Jesus' time. Jesus said that people's good works should glow as brightly as a lamp's precious light.

going to hell: membership in God's kingdom, he suggested, was worth this sacrifice.

Divorce, Jesus continued, was tantamount to turning the divorced woman into an adulteress. Later (Matthew 19:7–8), Jesus pointed out that although Moses had allowed divorce, this was because the people at that time were "hard-hearted." God's purpose, he said, was that male and female should become "one flesh."

Jesus then turned his attention to the traditional teaching on swearing. Whereas the Law insisted that a person should honor any oath they had sworn, Jesus said, "Do not swear at all… All you need say is 'Yes' if you mean yes, 'No' if you mean no." By this, Jesus seems to have been implying that if a person was honest, then oaths were unnecessary.

Perhaps the most challenging part of Jesus' sermon is his view on how to deal with violence. The Law had spoken of an "eye for eye and tooth for tooth [Exodus 21:24]," which was interpreted in Jesus' day as an accepted requirement to pay financial compensation for damage caused to another person.

It has been suggested that the Law originally was intended to set a limit on retribution. Jesus now told his followers that they must offer no resistance to violence. He also extended the traditional command to "love your neighbor" to enemies. Indeed, the early Christians, who themselves faced persecution by the Roman government, would have remembered that Jesus on the cross prayed for those who had caused his death: "Father, forgive them; they do not know what they are doing [Luke 23:34]."

✝ "Be perfect" ✝

The chapter ends with Jesus telling his disciples "to be perfect, just as your heavenly Father is perfect." This parallels the moment in the Old Testament when God called Israel to be holy: "I, Yahweh, your God, am holy [Leviticus 19:2]." Yet holiness for Israel had entailed separation from the non-Jews. Under God's new covenant, as manifested by Jesus, divisions were done away with and all people – Gentiles as well as Jews – were neighbors.

The Church of the Beatitudes in Galilee was built on the hilltop site where, according to local tradition, Jesus delivered his Sermon on the Mount.

Turning to religious behavior, Jesus warned against ostentatious displays of piety. Those who made a show of giving alms, he said, might receive the public acclaim they hoped for, but it would be their only reward. Those who, when giving alms, kept their generosity secret would be rewarded by their heavenly Father. Prayers, too, should not be uttered in public for show. Nor should people "babble as the Gentiles do." This behavior, Jesus said, showed a misunderstanding of the nature of God.

Jesus then recited a model prayer, which, as The Lord's Prayer, is known by heart by Christians around the world. The various petitions in the Lord's Prayer can be paralleled in Jewish writings, but there is no equivalent to the complete prayer. It begins with an address to God. The form in Luke (11:2–4) is simple. His version begins "Father," whereas Matthew's opens with the more respectful "Our Father in heaven."

The prayer then calls for the coming of God's kingdom and an affirmation of obedience to God's will. It continues with a request for bread – "Give us today our daily bread" – and so acknowledges that bodily sustenance comes from God. But it may also carry a reference to the

bread – representing the body of Christ – given at the Eucharist, Mass, or Communion service.

The petition for God's forgiveness – "And forgive us our debts, as we have forgiven those who are in debt to us" – is directly tied to human willingness to forgive. It implies that God's pardon is conditional on people forgiving others, but it is clear in Jesus' teachings that by fully accepting and appreciating divine mercy, people are bound to adopt an attitude of mercy to others. The prayer ends with a request not to be put to the test or, in some translations, not to be led

The flowers that Jesus said were sumptuously dressed by God are thought to be anemones such as these, which continue to grow in Palestine today.

"into temptation," and to be saved from the Evil One or evil – possibly a reference to the persecutions that could undermine people's faith.

After his teaching on prayer, Jesus returned to his point about avoiding public show and applied it to the practice of fasting – ritually abstaining from food. While some people, Jesus said, would make it known they were fasting by their gloomy appearance, the faithful should make sure that only God knew whether they were fasting.

Up to this point in the sermon, Jesus had taught about the inner motivation of his disciples' behavior toward other people and God. He then called for total trust in God's loving care. Storing up earthly treasure, he warned, not only showed a lack of confidence in God, but, because a person

would increasingly seek to keep his or her possessions safe from burglars and decay, it would also become a distraction. The disciples should not be anxious about food and clothing but trust fully in God: if God fed the birds, Jesus said, and dressed the flowers in clothes more beautiful than the royal robes of King Solomon, how much more would he look after the disciples?

Jesus also told his hearers to avoid judging others, so that God would not judge them. They should not worry about other people's behavior, but purify their own lives: if they were generous to others, they would receive generosity.

After an assurance that the prayers of the faithful would be answered by God, Jesus then summed up this part of his teaching with what Christians call the Golden Rule: "So always treat others as you would like them to treat you; that is the Law and the Prophets." By saying that this rule was the Law and the Prophets, Jesus was referring to his declaration that he had not come to abolish but to complete them (5:17).

✝ The two ways ✝

Jesus ended the sermon by warning that it is "a narrow gate and a hard road that leads to life," and false prophets might lead the faithful astray. A true prophet, he said, like a tree that bears good fruit, would be known by how he lived. Only those who did the will of God, not those who were vocal with their religious proclamations, would enter the kingdom of heaven.

Finally, Jesus told a story about a "sensible man" who built his house on rock and a "stupid man" who built his on sand. When the rain came and the floods rose and the gales blew, the house on the rock did not fall, but the stupid man's house collapsed. The rock was Jesus' teaching, the only sure foundation for life. He deeply impressed his audience, Matthew says, because he "taught them with authority, unlike their own scribes." He spoke with direct knowledge of the will of God, his heavenly Father. ❖

MESSAGE
—for—
TODAY

TOWARD THE END of his sermon, Jesus told his followers not to worry about their material existence — food, drink, clothes. He said that if God fed and clothed the animals and plants of the natural world, he would certainly make sure that his followers would not go without these basics.

The culture of the Western world places considerable emphasis on the desirability of material possessions. Magazines, billboards, television, and radio all urge people to adopt the latest fashion or buy the newest household appliances or automobiles. Yet material objects cannot in themselves bring happiness. Jesus said people could not serve both God and mammon (material wealth). They would inevitably love one and hate the other. Instead, he insisted, people should first seek the kingdom of heaven. As they did so, God would provide all they needed.

The BREAD of LIFE

The DISCOURSE at CAPERNAUM
JOHN 6:22–71

> " *I am the bread of life. No one who comes*
> *to me will ever hunger; no one who believes in me will*
> *ever thirst…I will certainly not reject*
> *anyone who comes to me…* "
>
> JOHN 6:35,37

OST OF JESUS' teachings in the Synoptic Gospels are told in the form of parables or short, meaning-laden sayings. Even the Sermon on the Mount (pp. 66–71) consists mainly of concise sayings collected around various themes. But in John's Gospel, a number of sermons, including the one Jesus told at Capernaum, combine concrete images with ideas that are more abstract.

According to John, Jesus went to Capernaum after he had fed a crowd of 5,000 people with only a few loaves of bread and a few fish. Having performed this miracle, he became alarmed that the people were going to force him to be their king, so he fled into the hills above the eastern coast of the Sea of Galilee. In the meantime, his disciples set out in a boat to return to Capernaum. They were later amazed to see Jesus walking across the lake to join them.

Back on the shore, the crowd also decided to make their way back to Capernaum to seek Jesus out. When they had reached the town and found him, Jesus told them that they wanted him only because he had satisfied their hunger with bread. He added that instead of working for food that went bad, they should work for food that endured – that is, to do the will of God. The people – who had apparently not recognized Jesus' miracle of the loaves and fish – asked him for a "sign," a word John uses to refer to a miracle. They pointed out to him that Moses, when leading the Children of Israel through the desert to the promised land of Canaan, had miraculously given them manna, or bread, from heaven (Exodus 16).

† Imperishable food †

Jesus then made two points. First, it was God, not Moses, who had provided manna. Second, God was now providing not perishable food but heavenly bread, in the person of his Son. When the crowd asked Jesus for this bread, he surprised them by saying – in the first of seven declarations about himself in John's Gospel – that he was "the bread of life." He made it clear that whoever ate this bread – that is, believed in him – would never be hungry, and no one would be turned away.

Jesus went on to say that he had come from heaven not to do his own will but that of his Father. These words would be echoed in his prayer in the Garden of Gethsemane, just before his arrest and crucifixion: addressing the Father, he said, "Let your will be done, not mine [Luke 22:42]." He added that all those who had faith in him would have eternal life.

On hearing Jesus' claim to be the "bread from heaven" and God's Son, his Jewish opponents argued among themselves. They believed that

The AD *fourth-century synagogue* at Capernaum, shown here with its remaining Corinthian columns, was built on top of a synagogue dating from Jesus' time that is thought to be where he gave his discourse.

Jesus was the son of Joseph – it was impossible for him to have come down from heaven. But Jesus told them to "stop complaining" – a reference that may have reminded John's readers of the mutterings of the Israelites against Moses (Numbers 14:1–4).

Reiterating that he was the bread of life, Jesus identified the bread with his flesh. He said that anyone who ate it would receive eternal life – not only life in the next world, but also a new quality of life in the present. In the final section of the sermon, Jesus declared that the only way to share

Jesus shares round loaves of bread – symbolizing spiritual sustenance – in this 15th-century painting of the Last Supper from Cyprus.

in the gift of eternal life was by eating his flesh and drinking his blood. Interpreting his words literally, many of his listeners were visibly disturbed, so Jesus repeated to them that it was not material things but the spirit that gave life, and his words were spirit.

✝ *Flesh and blood* ✝

Some scholars are surprised that although John's Gospel records Jesus teaching at his last meal with his disciples (13–17), it does not actually include an account of the institution of the Lord's Supper. Yet in Jesus' references to his flesh being "real food" and his blood being "real drink," early Christian readers would have

Stone mills such as this one, discovered in Palestine, would have been used to grind wheat into flour for making into bread in Jesus' time.

recognized the elements of the ritual meal – known now as Communion, Mass, or Eucharist – that commemorates this supper.

> ❝ *It is my Father's will that whoever sees the Son and believes in him should have eternal life…* ❞
>
> JOHN 6:40

After the sermon, aware that many of his followers were upset and had left him, Jesus asked his 12 disciples if they also intended to leave. Peter replied with the clearest confession of faith in Jesus anyone had yet made: "Lord, to whom shall we go…we have come to know that you are the Holy One of God." Jesus, however, warned that one of the 12 would betray him. Throughout his ministry, Jesus' presence caused division – among the Jews, his followers, and even his 12 disciples. ❖

MESSAGE — *for* — TODAY

MANY OF THOSE who listened to Jesus preach at Capernaum were baffled, disappointed, or even disgusted. Their inability to listen to new, challenging ideas or teachings with a mind free of prejudice closed their ears to one of the most profound pronouncements in human history.

In the past, religious reformers, such as the 16th-century German monk Martin Luther, have often been greeted with hostility. The history of science also shows the collision between religious orthodoxy and new discoveries. The 17th-century Italian scientist Galileo, for example, was forced by the church Inquisition to recant his support of the thesis that the Earth revolved around the Sun, not vice versa. Jesus' challenging teaching also aroused hostility. But for those who listened with open hearts his words were the gateway to spiritual rebirth.

The END of TIME

The SECOND COMING and the LAST JUDGMENT
MATTHEW 24:1–28

❝ *But anyone who stands firm to the end will be saved.*
This good news of the kingdom will be
proclaimed to the whole world as evidence to the
nations. And then the end will come. **❞**
MATTHEW 24:13–14

A S JESUS SAT in the Mount of Olives shortly before his death, he spoke to his disciples at length about the destruction of Jerusalem, the end of the world, and his own Second Coming (his return after death and resurrection to usher in the new order). He addressed them in front of the Temple, which had been rebuilt by Herod the Great, and alluding to its buildings, he predicted that the entire structure would be demolished: "Not a single stone here will be left on another: everything will be pulled down."

Jesus' words were later used against him at his trial (Matthew 26:61), a parallel to the situation some 600 years before, when the prophet Jeremiah had been threatened with death for his prediction that the First Temple would be destroyed (Jeremiah 26). Herod's Temple was, in fact, set on fire during the Romans' siege of Jerusalem in AD 70 and was subsequently leveled, along with the rest of the city.

✝ False prophets ✝

Jesus warned his disciples to beware of false prophets who came saying, "I am the Christ." There would be "wars and rumors of wars," he said, as well as earthquakes and famines. The faithful would suffer torture and even death, and many would lose their faith. Also, false prophets would appear, lawlessness would increase, and people's love for each other would "grow cold." The end, however, would not come until the good news of the kingdom had been proclaimed to the whole world.

Returning to predictions that disaster would soon befall Jerusalem, he advised his followers that when the time came they should drop everything and make their escape to the mountains. After another warning about the coming of false messiahs, Jesus echoed a passage from the Old Testament book of Daniel (7:13–14), predicting that at the end of the world the Son of man would come on the clouds of heaven with "great power and glory."

✝ The apocalyptic tradition ✝

During the centuries of oppression before the time of Jesus, when the Jewish people suffered at the hands of foreign powers, a form of literature known as "apocalyptic" – apocalypse means "revelation" – became common. These texts, whose authors wrote under pseudonyms, include the Book of Daniel; several of them, such as the Book of Enoch, were excluded from the Old Testament canon. References to war and persecutions, as well as to events heralding the

end of the world and the establishment of God's kingdom, were common apocalyptic themes, and Jesus followed this tradition in this discourse.

Yet Jesus avoided making specific prophecies about the date of his Second Coming. He said that neither he nor the angels in heaven knew when it would occur – only the Father knew (Matthew 24:36). In Acts, he told his disciples that it was not for them to know about dates and

Roman soldiers carry off a Jewish candlestick, or menorah, *after the sack of Jerusalem in* AD *70, in this relief from Titus' column in Rome. Shortly before his death, Jesus predicted the destruction of the city.*

times (1:7). In various parables, such as the Ten Wedding Attendants (pp. 58–59), he warned his disciples to be ever ready, because the Son of man would come at an hour they did not expect.

Many in the early church clearly felt Jesus' return to the world was imminent. Others thought that his predictions about his Second Coming were to some extent fulfilled at the feast of Pentecost (Acts 2:1–13), when his spirit filled and miraculously changed his disciples.

> ❝ *In truth I tell you…all these things will have taken place. Sky and earth will pass away, but my words will never pass away.* ❞
>
> MATTHEW 24:34-35

Some Christians today continue to speculate about the date of Christ's return. Many others, however, emphasize that, as the parable of the Sheep and the Goats (pp. 62–63) suggests, each moment may be a time when Jesus arrives, perhaps in the guise of someone who is needy. ❖

Jerusalem has had a turbulent history down to today. Occupied at various times by Romans, Muslims, and Crusader Christians, it is now held sacred by followers of Judaism, Christianity, and Islam.

MESSAGE
—for—
TODAY

IN DESCRIBING THE signs that would herald the end of the world, Jesus referred to the appearance of false messiahs and prophets who would lead people astray. For many Christians in modern times, the proliferation of cults and gurus in various parts of the Western world seem to be an eerie reminder of Jesus' words.

One of the characteristics of Western culture is that many people seek instant answers or quick fixes to rescue them from their spiritual malaise or other personal problems. Jesus did not promise any shortcuts to the kingdom of heaven. He stressed that commitment to God was a lifelong affair involving sacrifices, and that few would stay the course. But for the faithful there is no substitute for regular worship, prayer, contemplation, and acts of goodness, performed in a spirit of faith and humility.

THE CONVERSATIONS OF JESUS

LIKE SPIRITUAL TEACHERS from other religious traditions, Jesus not only taught through public addresses, but also through conversations with individuals. Sometimes these dialogues occurred through chance meetings. Sometimes people sought Jesus out. But no matter how the meetings came about, or whether the individuals were from the respectable or disreputable classes of society, Jesus was ready to challenge old ways of thinking and offer spiritual counsel.

During his life, Jesus must have had countless conversations, of which only a fraction were recorded in the Gospels. The most lengthy and significant occur in John's Gospel, where they often follow accounts of Jesus' miracles. Through them, it is possible to catch a revealing glimpse of a more intimate side of Jesus' character, and to understand how he encouraged a person's spiritual and moral growth. Talking to Nicodemus (pp. 80–83), who was one of the Pharisees, Jesus tried to explain how it was possible to be born again. In his conversation with a Samaritan woman (pp. 84–87), he described to her the difference between ordinary water and the "living water" that he was offering.

In his dialogue with the adulterous woman (pp. 88–89) and her accusers, Jesus taught that those who wish to enforce morality by punishment should recognize their own faults and remember the value of compassion. The last conversation (pp. 90–91) differs from the others, because it took place after the Resurrection, when Peter spoke to the Risen Jesus and Jesus charged him with the task of nurturing and leading the Christian faithful. ❖

An ENCOUNTER by NIGHT

NICODEMUS the PHARISEE

JOHN 3:1–21

> ❝ *'Rabbi, we know that you have come from God as a teacher; for no one could perform the signs that you do unless God were with him.'* ❞
>
> JOHN 3:2

SOME TIME WHEN Jesus was visiting Jerusalem, Nicodemus, a leading representative of the most pious of the Jews, the Pharisees, took the opportunity to visit Jesus at night in order to discover for himself exactly what this young Rabbi was like. Clearly, Nicodemus must have been impressed with Jesus' reputation as a spiritual teacher as well as a miracle worker. Yet John states that Nicodemus set out to see Jesus at night, which may suggest that while Nicodemus wanted to meet this extraordinary teacher, he was not ready to risk his reputation as a devout Jew by seeing Jesus openly, in public.

The meeting brought together two men, both teachers, one versed in the study of law, the other claiming the authority of spiritual experience. It took place soon after Jesus had expelled the money changers and traders from the Temple at Jerusalem. On that occasion, he had predicted that the Temple, the symbol of Judaism, would be replaced by the body of Christ. Now, in a conversation with Nicodemus, Jesus talked of the possibility of eternal life through belief in him, God's son.

Nicodemus began their talk by acknowledging Jesus as a teacher sent by God. Jesus replied that no one could see the kingdom of God without being "born from above," or born again. When Nicodemus protested that it was not possible for anyone to return to the womb and be reborn, Jesus told him that to enter God's kingdom, people had to be born through "water" – baptism – and the "Spirit." The Spirit, Jesus said, was like the wind, which blows where it wants and can be heard, but whose comings and goings cannot be seen. Nicodemus was still baffled, prompting Jesus to chide him with the words – possibly edged with irony – "You are the Teacher of Israel, and you do not know these things!"

✝ *The "fiery serpents"* ✝

Jesus continued to try to open his visitor's eyes. If Nicodemus did not grasp "earthly" or ordinary analogies, Jesus suggested, he would not understand it when Jesus spoke of "heavenly things." Jesus then rehearsed with Nicodemus something Israel's teacher would know well – Jewish history. Remember the time, he said, when the Israelites, traveling through the wilderness toward the Promised Land, had offended God. God punished them by sending "fiery serpents" whose bites could be fatal. The people soon repented of their sins, and God instructed Moses, their leader, to make a bronze serpent and lift it up, so that those who had been bitten could survive their wounds by looking at the effigy, and remember God's mercy (Numbers 21:4–9).

Jesus compared this to the time when he would be lifted up on the cross, when all who looked on him would see God's love in action and receive the gift of eternal life.

Jesus told Nicodemus that through his love for the world, God had given his only Son so that people might be saved. His Son had not come to judge people, but those who did not believe in him would automatically be judged, because they preferred "darkness to the light" – a phrase that might have unsettled Jesus' visitor, who had sought a nighttime meeting. Jesus then ended the

Nicodemus the Pharisee (right) listens to Jesus during a nighttime visit, in this 16th-century Dutch painting. Jesus took the opportunity to enlighten a man who was well-versed in the Jewish law but slow in understanding the workings of the Holy Spirit.

conversation by saying that those who did evil hated exposure to the light, but those who lived in truth came out into the light so that their deeds "may plainly appear as done in God."

In the discourses and conversations John included in his Gospel, he often contrasted Jesus' teaching with that of the Jewish leaders. This may have been especially relevant by the time he wrote his Gospel – probably at about the end of the first century – because followers of Jesus and those of the Jewish faith were both claiming exclusively to be the one true people of God.

✝ A spiritual rebirth ✝

John suggests that the "Jews" – a collective term he applied to Jesus' opponents – judged people and situations by worldly standards and consistently misunderstood Jesus by taking his remarks literally. Nicodemus gave a typically literal interpretation to what Jesus said about being "born from above." In fact, Jesus was referring to a spiritual, not a physical, rebirth. When Jesus returned to his theme about the need to be born "through water and the Spirit," John's readers would have recalled the rites of baptism and confirmation.

Jesus tried to illuminate the nature of the Spirit by likening it to the wind; the Greek word for wind, *pneuma*, also means "spirit." Just as the wind is observed only by its effects, so a spiritual rebirth is observed only in the quality of a person's life. Membership in God's kingdom

This lamplit passageway in Jerusalem would have been the type of street Nicodemus walked along to visit Jesus. His journey perhaps symbolizes the path from darkness to the light of spiritual understanding.

depends on this, Jesus stated, not on physical birth, which was the natural basis for membership of the Chosen People of Israel.

† Jesus' exaltation †

Nicodemus was even more puzzled by Jesus' comparison between the Spirit and wind. Here, the difference between head knowledge and spiritual experience became obvious. Jesus spoke of what he knew and had seen to a man who had only education. What was witnessed to was the Son of man, through whom God showed his love for the world. John uses the title Son of man to stress Jesus' humanity, often with reference to Jesus' crucifixion, which John describes as the "lifting up" or "exaltation" of Jesus.

> **“** He gave his only Son, so that everyone who believes in him may… have eternal life. **”**
>
> JOHN 3:16

Jesus told Nicodemus that the purpose of the Son of man's death would be the salvation of all who believed in him. It was the expression of God's love for the world – that is, for all people, not just a chosen group. Judgment, Jesus said, was not something God inflicted, but what people brought upon themselves by refusing divine love.

John does not state whether Nicodemus remained in the darkness of the night or came to recognize Jesus as the light of the world. However, he does say that on a later occasion, among other Pharisees, Nicodemus argued that Jesus deserved a fair trial (7:50–52).

After the crucifixion it was Nicodemus who went with Joseph of Arimathea to ask Pontius Pilate for the body of Jesus and assisted with his burial (19:38–42). It is a reasonable speculation that a record of this conversation would not have been made unless Nicodemus had shared it with the first believers. ❖

MESSAGE —for— TODAY

JESUS THREW Nicodemus off balance when he told him that it was necessary to be born again. Nicodemus could not grasp that Jesus was referring to a spiritual birth – the emergence of a "new" person directed by the Holy Spirit.

For many who live their lives without any spiritual nourishment, a time comes when they experience an existential crisis. They wonder whether the world is really just a conglomeration of atoms, devoid of any spiritual purpose. Possibly it was a personal crisis – perhaps a sense of his spiritual limitations – that made Nicodemus seek out Jesus. Jesus addressed his message to all searchers of truth – irrespective of their age, status, or color. The only precondition he set was an attitude of faith that, through him, God's love would flow into people's hearts and make them new.

At JACOB'S WELL

The WOMAN of SAMARIA
JOHN 4:1–42

" *The water that I shall give…will become…a spring of water within, welling up for eternal life.* "
JOHN 4:14

ONE OF THE most evocative conversations Jesus is recorded to have had took place when Jesus was passing through Samaria on his way from Judea to Galilee. Jesus sat down to rest at "Jacob's well," situated by the town of Sychar, near where the Jewish patriarch Jacob had given land to his son Joseph, according to the Old Testament (Genesis 48:22).

John's readers would certainly have appreciated the well's associations. It was Jacob – whose name was later changed to Israel – who dreamed of a ladder leading up to heaven from Earth. Earlier in John's account, Jesus had used the metaphor of that ladder to describe the Son of man (John 1:51). It was an appropriate place, therefore, for the person whom John believed to be the true heir of Jacob to stop.

At the "sixth hour" – midday – a Samaritan woman arrived at the well to fetch some water. The Jews and the Samaritans did not associate with each other because of past enmities (pp. 22–25). When Jesus asked her to give him something to drink, she was taken aback because she recognized him as a Jew.

Responding to her surprise, Jesus offered her "living water." Again she was perplexed because she could see clearly that Jesus did not have a bucket, and she interpreted his words literally. In the Old Testament, "living water" often signifies divine activity (Jeremiah 2:13). Here, John intended it to symbolize the Holy Spirit – he later explains Jesus' words, "Let anyone who is thirsty come to me," with the comment, "He was speaking of the Spirit, which those who believed in him were to receive [7:39]."

† The spring of water †

Jesus told her that those who drank water from a well would inevitably be thirsty again. But the water he was offering to her would quench a person's thirst forever – it would become "a spring of water, welling up for eternal life." The woman replied, perhaps sarcastically, that she wanted the water he offered to save her from the daily drudgery of drawing it.

Jesus asked the woman to call her husband. She answered that she had no husband. Jesus, with the supernatural insight John was certain he possessed, said her reply was true; she had had five husbands, and the man she was now with was not her husband. John does not say whether her previous husbands had died or divorced her. Certainly, contemporary Jewish rabbis did not approve of more than three marriages, although any number was legally admissible.

The woman was evidently not legally married to the man she was then with. Jesus' knowledge of the intimacies of her life deeply impressed the woman. "I see you are a prophet," she said, perhaps trying to change the direction of an increasingly uncomfortable exchange. She then pointed out to Jesus that the Samaritans worshiped on "this

mountain" – Mount Gerizim – whereas the Jews insisted that the only place for worship was in the city of Jerusalem.

Jesus bowed to her diversionary tactic with two telling points. First, the Jews knew the God whom they worshiped, whereas the Samaritans did not. In fact, salvation would come from the Jews. Second, a time was coming when people

Jesus talks to the Samaritan woman, who has come to fetch water from the well, in this painting by the 19th-century British artist George Richmond.

would worship neither on Mount Gerizim nor in Jerusalem: geographical location was ultimately irrelevant because God was "spirit, and those who worship must worship in spirit and truth."

By this point, the woman must have felt out of her depth. She answered simply that when the Messiah came, he would explain everything. With equal simplicity, Jesus replied, "That is who I am, I who speak to you." The English translation, however, does not emphasize the great importance of the phrase "I am." In the Old Testament, God named Himself "I am" when He told Moses to say to the Israelites, "I am has sent me to you [Exodus 3:14]."

At this moment, Jesus' disciples returned from buying food and saw with surprise that he talked to the woman. She promptly went back to

A Palestinan woman draws water from a well next to her tent. Although well water was – and is – crucial in a hot, arid land, Jesus told the woman of Samaria that this water would never fully quench her thirst.

Sychar. The disciples urged Jesus to eat, but found that he was not hungry – he said he had "food to eat that you do not know about." When they took his words literally, Jesus explained that his real sustenance was to do the will of God, who had sent him and whose work was now coming to fruition. It would be the disciples' work to reap many converts after the efforts of those who had labored to sow before them – a reference, perhaps, to the Old Testament prophets or to John the Baptist.

† The Samaritans' faith †

Meanwhile, many Samaritans in Sychar had been persuaded by the woman's story to believe in Jesus' spiritual status and had come out to urge him to stay with them for a while. Jesus

A tributary of the Jordan River gushes powerfully over rocks – a physical reminder that Jesus called himself "the living water" that gave eternal life.

agreed to stay for two days. After meeting Jesus face to face, many more believed that he was the "Savior of the world."

> ❝ But the hour is coming –
> indeed is already
> here – when true worshipers
> will worship the Father in
> spirit and truth: that
> is the kind of worshiper the
> Father seeks. ❞
>
> JOHN 4:23

The Samaritans recognized that in Jesus the distinction between Jew and Samaritan was abolished. Although John presents Jesus as the Jewish Messiah, he makes it clear that Jesus is the "Savior of the world" – a title that was applied to some Roman Emperors. John was claiming not only that the various contemporary expressions of religious life had been superseded by Jesus, but also that true power resided in him (John 19:11). ❖

MESSAGE
—for—
TODAY

TALKING TO the Samaritan woman, Jesus showed that he did not hesitate to engage in conversation someone whose race, gender, and marital – or lack of marital – status naturally made her a social outcast in the eyes of a pious Jew. He made it clear that social mores had their limits. In a similar vein, he indicated that traditional places of worship were of limited value: God was a spirit, and people must worship God "in spirit and truth."

The world would be a less colorful place if all the cathedrals, mosques, and temples had never been built. But Jesus suggested that people should not be dependent on places of worship and their physical or ritual trappings. God does not relate to people only among the pews of churches or the statues of Hindu temples. He is spirit, Jesus said, and can be worshiped in any place on Earth.

CASTING *the* FIRST STONE

The ADULTEROUS WOMAN

JOHN 7:53–8:11

❝ Woman, where are they?
Has no one condemned you? ❞

JOHN 8:10

THE STORY OF the adulterous woman is one of the more problematic passages in the Bible, because the verses that recount it are omitted in most of the oldest biblical manuscripts. All four of the earliest codices – copies of the New Testament bound in book form – omit the passage, although it is included in the late fifth-century Codex Bezae, as well as in other later manuscripts. In some of these, the story is placed in Luke's Gospel. Certainly the form and style are more reminiscent of the Synoptic Gospels than of

John, yet the story seems true both to the character and teaching of Jesus and to John's emphasis on personal encounters.

The story is set in the Temple at Jerusalem, where Jesus was preaching. The scribes and Pharisees brought to him a woman who had been caught committing adultery. They informed Jesus that the Law of Moses ordered the stoning of

Jesus challenges the accusers eager to punish the adulterous woman, who kneels down, in this painting by the 17th-century French artist Nicholas Poussin.

adulterous women and asked him what his view was. According to Jewish Law, a woman already engaged who had intercourse with another man was to be stoned (Deuteronomy 22:23–24). At the time of Jesus, however, such executions would have been rare, since the Romans evidently prohibited Jews from carrying out capital penalties (John 18:31).

✝ Writing on the ground ✝

The scribes and the Pharisees had confronted Jesus with a dilemma. If Jesus said the woman should be stoned, he could be reported to the Romans for flouting their authority. But if he told them to let her go, he could be accused of moral laxity and flouting the teaching of Moses.

While they waited for his response, Jesus bent down and wrote on the ground with his finger. Scholars continue to debate the meaning of this gesture, and John offers no clues as to its relevance. He then told the woman's accusers: "Let the one among you who is guiltless be the first to throw a stone at her." Jesus need not have been implying that all the woman's accusers had themselves committed adultery. The word "guiltless" means "innocent." He suggested that anyone who was totally innocent of all sin should throw the first stone: but the only one who was wholly innocent was Jesus, the Son of God.

Having given his verdict, Jesus continued to write on the ground. The accusers had no answer – they did not dare to claim themselves sinless. Neither could they, any more than Jesus, flout Roman law. Instead, they slunk away, one by one. Left alone with the woman, Jesus asked her where her accusers had gone. When she replied that no one had condemned her, Jesus answered, "Neither do I condemn you. Go away, and from this moment sin no more." Jesus refused to act as a judge, declaring her guilty or innocent. But his injunction to "sin no more" carried the warning that adultery had no part in the way of righteous living he was preaching. ❖

MESSAGE
—for—
TODAY

THOSE WHO brought the adulterous woman before Jesus were ready to publicly condemn and shame her for her immoral behavior. Jesus clarified the situation by turning the accusers back on themselves, forcing them to ponder their own morality.

Among the attitudes Jesus denounced, self-righteousness ranked high. It bespoke a deadly level of pride and a lack of forgiveness that had no place in the kingdom of God. That the accusers had ulterior motives made their actions all the more ugly. In the same way that Jesus told the woman's accusers to examine their own moral conduct, it behooves us all, whenever we feel the urge to find fault in someone, to stop and look at ourselves — in terms both of character and motive. Only by appreciating our own deficiencies will we feel compassion for others' failings.

MEETING *the* RISEN JESUS

The CHARGE *to* PETER

JOHN 21:15–19

> **❝** *'Simon, son of John, do you love me?'*
> *He replied, 'Yes, Lord, you know I love you.'* **❞**
>
> JOHN 21:16

SOME TIME AFTER Jesus' death and resurrection, Peter and the other disciples returned from Jerusalem to Galilee, to take up their old work as fishermen. At the end of an unsuccessful night's fishing, a mysterious figure appeared on the shore and instructed them to throw their nets to starboard. When they did as they were bidden, they caught an enormous haul of fish. For Peter, this was a familiar miracle (Luke 5:1–6) and he instantly realized that the figure was Jesus. Coming ashore, the disciples breakfasted with Jesus, whom they all now could see was the Risen Lord.

After breakfast, Jesus addressed Peter by his original name, saying, "Simon, son of John, do you love me more than these others do?" This question must have carried a sting in it's tail, because Peter had earlier boasted (Matthew 26:33) that

even if all the others fell away, he would not do so. Peter simply said, "Lord, you know I love you," to which Jesus replied, "Feed my lambs."

Jesus repeated the question and Peter answered as before, prompting Jesus to say, "Look after my sheep." When Jesus asked the question for a third time, Peter was hurt and answered: "Lord, you know everything, you know I love you." Again Jesus said, "Feed my sheep." Some scholars point out that Peter, in his reply, uses a different word for love (*philein*) than that used by Jesus (*agapan*) in his first two questions. Because *philein* carries the sense of human, as opposed to divine, love, it may be a further sign of Peter's new humility: whereas before he had been too

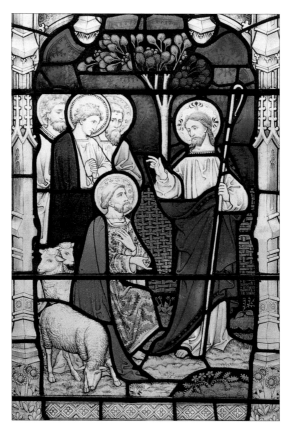

Jesus, depicted as a shepherd holding a crook, charges Peter to "feed my sheep" – the Christian faithful – in this 19th-century British stained-glass window.

confident of his steadfastness, now he was not prepared to commit himself to the divine love that Jesus embodied in his life and works.

Jesus warned Peter of the price the disciple would pay for faithfulness. As a young man he had walked where he liked; as an old man he would stretch out his hands and have a belt put around him and be taken to where he "would rather not go." This was an allusion, as John points out, to Peter's death by crucifixion, which probably occurred during the persecution of the Christians by the Roman emperor Nero in AD 64. By this death, John declared, Peter would "give glory to God."

✝ Peter's denial ✝

The conversation between Jesus and Peter – traditionally known as the Charge to Peter – concerns the future ministry of Jesus' foremost disciple. The brother of Andrew, Peter was originally called Simon. Jesus renamed him Cephas, or Peter (the Aramaic and Greek names for Rock), on whose faith, Jesus declared, the Church would be founded.

An energetic, impetuous man, Peter became a leader and spokesman for the disciples. But his faith and courage sometimes deserted him. In fact, in Peter's threefold affirmation of love toward Jesus, most scholars see a parallel with the occasion when Peter denied Jesus three times after Jesus was arrested (John 18:15 ff).

On the other side of the resurrection, it was as if Jesus were healing Peter's wounds from his previous frailty. At the same time, he commanded him to feed his lambs or sheep – that is, to nurture and lead the Christian faithful.

Jesus ended the conversation with the words "follow me," words that recalled the first time he had met Peter, also by the Sea of Galilee, and had recruited him as a disciple. Here, the suggestion is that Peter, having learned to rely not on his own strength but that of his Lord, was ready to care for others and follow Jesus to his own death. ❖

MESSAGE
—for—
TODAY

WHEN PETER spoke to the Risen Christ by the Sea of Galilee, he must have suffered with memories of times in the past when his courage and faith had deserted him. His previous failures, it seems, were a necessary step by which he gained the humility and strength to lead the first Christians.

The ancient Greeks used the word hubris to describe the arrogance of humans who were dismissive of the power of the gods and thought they could achieve everything by their own strength. In Greek myth and literature, hubris usually resulted in death or disaster. Jesus constantly acknowledged the fact that his power came from God, not himself. He made it clear that the faithful could live effectively only by recognizing their limitations and inviting the Holy Spirit to work through them.

BIBLIOGRAPHY

Argyle, A.W. *The Gospel According to Matthew.* Cambridge University Press, Cambridge 1963

Barclay, William *And He Had Compassion.* St. Andrews Press, Edinburgh, 1970
– *Gospel of Matthew.* St. Andrews Press, Edinburgh, 1975
– *Gospel of Mark.* St. Andrews Press, Edinburgh, 1975
– *Gospel of Luke.* St. Andrews Press, Edinburgh, 1975
– *Gospel of John.* St. Andrews Press, Edinburgh, 1975

Barrett, C.K. *The Gospel According to St. John.* SPCK, London, 1962

Brown, Raymond E. *The Community of the Beloved Disciple.* Paulist Press, New York, 1979

Caird, G.B. *St. Luke.* Penguin, London, 1963

Conzelmann, H. *An Outline of the Theology of the New Testament.* SCM Press Ltd., London, 1969

Dodd, C.H. *The Parables of the Kingdom.* James Nisbet and Co., London, 1935; Revised Edition, Fontana/Collins, London, 1961

Donahue, J.R. *The Gospel in Parable.* Fortress Press, Minneapolis, 1967

Drury, John *The Parables in the Gospels: History and Allegory.* SPCK, London, 1985

Evans, C.F. *St. Luke.* SCM Press Ltd., London, 1990

Fenton, J.C. *Saint Matthew.* Penguin, London, 1963
– *The Gospel According to John.* Clarendon Press, Oxford, 1970

Grant, R.M. *A Historical Introduction to the New Testament.* Collins, London, 1971

Hendrickx, Herman *The Parables of Jesus.* Chapman, London, 1986

Hunter, A.M. *Interpreting the Parables.* SCM Press Ltd., London, 1960
– *The Parables, Then and Now.* SCM Press Ltd, London, 1971

Jeremias, Joachim *The Parables of Jesus.* SCM Press Ltd., London, 1963
– *Rediscovering the Parables.* SCM Press Ltd., London, 1978

Jones, Geraint Vaughan *The Art and Truth of the Parables.* SCM Press Ltd., London 1963

Koester, Helmut *Ancient Christian Gospels.* SCM Press Ltd., London, 1990

Linneman, Eta *The Parables of Jesus.* SPCK, London, 1966

Lightfoot, R.H. *St. John's Gospel.* Oxford University Press, Oxford, 1956

Marsh, John *Saint John.* Penguin, London, 1968

Nineham, D.E. *Saint Mark.* Penguin, London, 1963

Perrin, Norman *The Kingdom of God in the Teaching of Jesus.* SCM Press Ltd., London, 1963

Rawlinson, E.J. *The Gospel According to St. Mark.* Methuen, London, 1925

Riches, John *The World of Jesus.* Cambridge University Press, Cambridge, 1990

Sanders, E.P. *Jesus and Judaism.* SCM Press Ltd., London, 1985

Scott, B.B. *Hear Then The Parables.* Fortress Press, Minneapolis, 1988

Taylor, Vincent *The Gospel According To St. Mark.* Macmillan, London, 1963

Temple, William *Readings in St. John's Gospel.* Macmillan, London, 1961

INDEX

ACKNOWLEDGMENTS

ILLUSTRATION

Debbie Hinks (illustration symbols).

PICTURE CREDITS

l = left, **r** = right

1 Laura Lushington/Sonia Halliday Photographs; **2-3** Jon Arnold Photography; **5-7** Sonia Halliday Photographs; **8** Robert Harding Picture Library; **11** National Gallery of Art, Washington/AKG London; **12** Zefa Picture Library; **13** Shai Ginott/ASAP/Robert Harding Picture Library; **14** Laura Lushington/Sonia Halliday Photographs; **16** Moira Savonius/ NHPA; **17** Tony Stone Images; **18** Laura Lushington/Sonia Halliday Photographs; **20** Jon Arnold; **23** Forbes Magazine Collection/Bridgeman Art Library; **24** Robert Harding Picture Library; **25** Laura Lushington/ Sonia Halliday Photographs; **26** Bridgeman Art Library; **29** Sonia Halliday Photographs; **30** Ancient Art & Architecture Collection; **33** Kunsthistorisches Museum, Vienna/Bridgeman Art Library; **34l** Matt Bain/NHPA, **34r** Alberto Nardi/NHPA; **36** Sonia Halliday Photographs; **38** York City Art Gallery/ Bridgeman; **40** Peter Clayton; **42** Laura Lushington/Sonia Halliday Photographs; **45** Sonia Halliday Photographs; **46** Giraudon/Bridgeman Art Library; **49** Michael Busselle/ Tony Stone Images; **50** Henry Ausloos/ NHPA; **51** Sonia Halliday Photographs; **53** AKG, London; **54** Paul Solomon/ Wheeler Pictures/Colorific!; **56** Christie's Images; **58** Angelo Hornak/National Trust Photographic Library; **60** Sonia Halliday Photographs; **63** Bridgeman Art Library; **64** Jon Arnold Photography; **67** Bridgeman Art Library; **68** Ancient Art & Architecture Collection; **69** Jon Arnold Photography; **70** Robert Harding Picture Library; **73** Jon Arnold Photography; **74** Sonia Halliday Photographs; **75** Jon Arnold Photography; **77** Ancient Art & Architecture Collection; **78** Jon Arnold Photography; **81** Christie's Images; **82** E. Simanor/Robert Harding Picture Library; **85** Tate Gallery Publications; **86** Sonia Halliday Photographs; **87** Jon Arnold Photography; **88** Erich Lessing/AKG London; **90** Laura Lushington/Sonia Halliday Photographs; **96** Jon Arnold Photography.

If the publishers have unwittingly infringed copyright in any of the illustrations reproduced, they would pay an appropriate fee on being satisfied of the owner's title.

*A **modern sculpture** of Jesus blessing Peter marks the spot traditionally held to be where they met by the Sea of Galilee after Jesus' resurrection.*